Strategic Software Quality Management

This book introduces strategic management tools and techniques appropriate for use in software quality management. There has been a gap between strategic management and software quality, and the solutions for solving the problems and improving the software quality usually come from the experience of IT experts: the managerial experience. This book helps people interested in software quality to go beyond the IT technical issues and integrate strategic management tools with their technical knowledge to become more prepared for the future, develop long-term plans for solutions and improvements, take more strategic decisions even when compared with the competitors, and finally, reach sustainable continuous improvements.

This book, by bridging software quality management and strategic management, can be used by software quality practitioners for effective results. The software development process is usually studied with regards to its functional aspects and the attempts to improve the quality and performance are mainly concentrated on the technical side. The developers, testers, or engineers search for solutions mostly directed toward a local problem specific to a unit, department, or code. What is often missing is grasping the big image of the problem: the managerial aspect. Even if all the technical staff are doing their tasks as they were planned, there is a vital need for identifying the bottlenecks and the points in need of improvements, alterations, and exclusions, together with tracking the progress and coming up with future strategies. This makes the software quality management activities intertwined with the strategic management concepts where strategic management enhances the quality management with its tools and techniques, and, in return, the software quality management provides the strategic management with insights on the technical issues, resulting in symbiosis. The highly competitive nature of the IT world makes it inevitable to take strategic tools and techniques into account and infuse them into the technical practices of software quality management.

This book encompasses the following chapters: analyzing the current situation, identifying the improvement areas, determining the strategies, tracking the progress, and achieving a sustainable improvement.

Strategic Software Quality Management

How to Incorporate Sustainable Continuous Improvement Practices

Mahsa Fidanboy and Cemalettin Öcal Fidanboy

Routledge
Taylor & Francis Group
A PRODUCTIVITY PRESS BOOK

First published 2025
by Routledge
605 Third Avenue, New York, NY 10158
and by Routledge

4 Park Square, Milton Park, Abingdon, Oxon, OX14 4RN

Routledge is an imprint of the Taylor & Francis Group, an informa business

ISBN: 9781032793627 (hbk)
ISBN: 9781032793610 (pbk)
ISBN: 9781003491606 (ebk)

DOI: 10.4324/9781003491606

Typeset in Garamond
by KnowledgeWorks Global Ltd.

To my all, my son, Vedat Ozan
and
my grandparents, Babaji and Mamaryam,
my mom, my sister, and my husband.
(Mahsa Fidanboy)

Contents

About the Authors

Dr. Mahsa Fidanboy has been active in the IT sector for over 10 years, primarily focusing on agile methods, software development standards and models, health information systems, and IT service management. During her graduate studies, she specialized in information systems and R&D performance. She is the author of the book *Organizations and Complex Adaptive Systems*. She has attained international certifications in project management, agile methods, telecommunications, sustainability, and IT-related frameworks and models. Additionally, she has held various positions as a trainer, consultant, sustainability expert, and quality expert.

Dr. Cemalettin Öcal Fidanboy, with a career spanning over 25 years, has held roles as a software quality manager and IT management consultant across various public and private organizations. He has taught courses in software quality management, management information systems, organizational theory, and R&D management at several universities, both as a part-time instructor and a full-time faculty member. Additionally, he provides consultancy and training in IT management, agile practices, software processes, and project management. He holds the title of Associate Professor and currently serves as a faculty member at OSTIM Technical University.

Chapter 1

Analyzing the Situation

1.1 Introduction

Before starting any actions and making any decisions, the current situation should always be investigated well, considering all the factors that play roles in the existence, occurrence, or reoccurrence of the situation.

The main problem that we face in the software development processes is that knowing the whole process in detail is not feasible, but hardly probable. It needs so much effort and time. For this reason, different parts of the processes are assigned to different experts, and when it comes to the decision-making time, some communicate with the other process experts to gain a bigger image and a holistic view of the problem; however, IT people, if we may label them this way, may in most cases prefer to avoid communication, and for this reason, the decisions that are made may not be the best choices. This problem is very common and the possibility of another choice that can be more appropriate is overseen. To overcome the two widely encountered problems, having required information on just part of the processes and a lack of efficient communication, methods used for the analysis of the current situation become of great significance. Communication was accompanied by the word "efficient" due to the fact that in many cases, communication is taking place but it is not performed in the correct ways. There are so many reasons for the inefficient communication. Some of them are:

- Asking the wrong questions.
- Focusing on the width of issues instead of the depth of issues.

DOI: 10.4324/9781003491606-1

- Getting distracted by arising questions.
- Being unable to narrow down the problems to a specific question or questions.

Given all those were mentioned, asking questions can be called "the art of asking questions."

At the first step of analyzing the current situation, we focus on this practice. The chapter continues with cases, pushes readers toward the real world, and expects him/her to produce ideas for solving the problems. The book recommends methods and/or techniques related to each case.

1.2 Evaluating the Current Situation

Performing the analysis of the current situation begins with asking the right questions. Just like theoretical research, which is expected to start from a research question, the importance of asking the right question should not be neglected in practice as well.

We all know that the question leads to the answer, which then results in the formation of the solution to the problem. Therefore, taking our time to define the questions should neither be taken as a waste of time nor as an individual isolated activity or task. The time spent for question definition can be included in the solution planning time within the context of projects. Let us take a look at the ways and methods to enhance and strengthen our art of asking questions.

Figure 1.1 shows the overall image of what is recommended here for analyzing the existing situation.

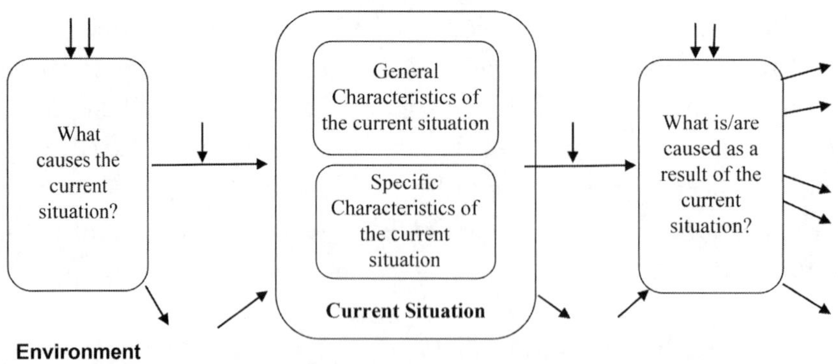

Figure 1.1 Current situation analysis.

What is meant by general characteristics of a situation is about being able to explain the situation simply to a nontechnical person. On the contrary, the technical aspect is the part that can be explained to and comprehended by a technical person and is called as the specific characteristics of the situation here.

From the other perspective, the nontechnical aspect is the explanation of the problem in general, in a manner that a person from another sector, with another expertise or professional background, can grasp the main points.

There are popular methods and techniques that are widely used for learning about a situation. These should be tailored based on the needs of the user and the context in which the method is applied. Let's take a look at some of these techniques.

5W1H method is a method widely used due to its simplicity of use and applicability to different contexts. As it can be understood from its name, it consists of asking five questions starting with W and a question starting with H. The question words are: where, who, when, which, what, and how.

What makes this method valuable and popular is aiming at different aspects of a problem while forcing the respondent to provide answers beyond "yes" and "no," which are preferred by respondents whenever they want to escape from explaining the details, for many reasons.

NOTES

Our experience shows that the common source of problems in software companies is people problems. The reasons behind the problems based on our observations can be listed this way:

- *Lack of required knowledge concerning the problem. In such cases, the employee is unable to show the knowledge he/she is expected to possess.*
- *Lack of the technical skill to solve the problem. Most of the cases deal with employees who have not refreshed their skill relevant to the usage of tools or their incompetency to keep their technical skill updated with new solutions.*
- *This will be the case for most fields in the near future since the ability to integrate the daily tasks with AI will be the new minimum for most jobs.*

- *Unable to assign the problem to an individual due to resource scarcity. Labor force particularly in software development is not limited within geographical borders. In IT sector, many individuals have started to work remotely during the pandemic and the same work model has been preferred by many ever since. This may raise the question of how we face resource scarcity. The answers can be condensed into two phrases: qualified resource scarcity and unreal compensation expectation of the unemployed individuals.*
- *Unable to allocate the necessary time to the problem because of the time pressure. What is seen is that usually estimations are not correctly done or done at all at the beginning of a project and this results in the human resources to work extra hours to catch the deadlines. There are not a few situations where an employee is working 8–9 hours a day and the following week he/she is searching for a task to do. Therefore, estimation and planning should not be underestimated in projects.*

Companies can benefit from qualitative data collection methods in extracting problems from their processes.

Qualitative Research Methods are the methods utilized for investigating the depth of the problems, unveiling the unseen aspects of the contexts, and going far behind the math of the issues. The most common qualitative data collection methods are:

- In-depth interviews.
- Focus groups.
- Participant observation.

The analytical objectives of qualitative research can be: explaining variation, describing relationships, outlining the individual experiences, and depicting the group norms, whereas the aims of quantitative research were stated as: measuring variation, forecasting causal relationships, and explaining a population's characteristics (Mack et al., 2005).

These methods specifically collecting data from focus groups are popular among software companies.

The Focus Group consists of 3–12 people and a moderator who is responsible for ensuring that the discussion focuses on the topic.

Several steps were noted for focus group research:

- Defining the research question.
- Plan the schedule and the structure of the session; usually takes 2–3 hours.
- Choosing the group, which depends on the topic and the kind of information needed to be gathered.
- Holding the focus group event (Kontio et al., 2004).

Some of the applications are risk management, requirement prioritization, and usability evaluation studies (Kontio et al., 2004); root cause determination; new feature development; and new tool evaluation. It has been long used as a tool for marketing to learn about the opinions and ideas regarding a new product. Software companies may employ this method for discovering innovative ideas, developing new software, adding features to new software, diagnosing the problems and issues with the current software, and uncovering a niche in the market. Although widely implemented, many incorrect ways of employing the tool are seen.

NOTES

Our observations from software companies reveal that the problem with the focus group method execution is that the lengthy tedious sessions sometimes take as long as a working day or two. This might be due to not predefining the topic exactly and/or not limiting the discussion to a specific number of issues that can be covered in the given time.

The other reason may be the inexperience of the moderator who could not manage the session, and keeping the dialogue centered on the topic.

In an interesting paper published in 2003, the software process improvement (SPI) problems of several software companies were studied by collecting data from focus groups and the identified issues were categorized under three groups: organizational, project-related, and software-related, which are further divided into 16 sub-groups (Beecham et al., 2003). The findings of their research depicted that the capability maturity of a company is in relation with the category of the issues it is involved with.

Case 1 – Company A has adopted the agile methodology for all its projects. Despite the tremendous amount of time and effort spent to train the employees on the methodology, the myths of agile are affecting the practices of most of the teams. Some of the problems are:

- No planning and estimation are done.
- No documentation is prepared and maintained.
- Lengthy meetings are held under the name of "daily meetings" and employees are stressed out and worried about the time they lost due to these meetings.
- The problems mentioned are common to many companies and projects. The predicted benefits of agile, of which its most important one is to get the customers involved in the project and to move forward based on their needs, are not achieved, and what it ends with is the burnout of the people on the project and the constant chaos originating from the constant changes.
- Now, suppose that you are a consultant hired by company A to solve the problems.

NOTES

It should never be forgotten that there is not only one solution to a case. There may be many options and the solutions may hold similarities and differences from each other. However, the wise thing to do is to be a good listener, a good researcher, a good scribe, and a good analyst.

Listening to every detail the people on the project share is of great importance. Sometimes, you can pretend to be busy taking notes, so that they continue explaining the problems in more detail. The hidden stories behind the toughest scenarios are mostly reached this way!

Search for the same or similar scenarios on the internet, ask your colleagues, ask the people on the project the questions of "what do you think can be done to fix this problem?" and continue with asking more detailed questions as the respondents keep on elaborating on the solutions.

Being a good scribe has always been of great importance as what is remembered after meetings can be interpreted in an incorrect way later. The best scribe is what is both comprehensive and brief at the same time; not too lengthy or too short. Maintaining this balance needs practice.

Analyzing can be a talent, but at the same time, a skill which can be learned. Try developing your analyzing skills by doing practice. The analyst should ask himself/herself these three questions first:

- *What do I have as the data?*
- *What can I do with these data?*
- *What can be gained after analysis? Or what is the fruit of this analysis?*

These three questions are for the situations where the data were collected and handed to the analyst. Before coming to this stage, the analyst should plan for the type of data required to be collected based on the context, goal, and method. Unfortunately, the companies collect data and then hire or hold analyst responsible for analyzing them, overlooking the fact that the analysis is dependent on the data, and for this reason, the analyst needs to specify the decisions on data collection at the beginning of each project.

Going back to our Company A case, applying the 5W1H method can lead to such questions:

- Where does the problem rest for the lack of planning and estimation?
- Who is responsible for doing the planning and estimation of the project?
- When should the planning and estimation be done in the project?
- Which kind of projects (similarities between them) mostly lack planning and estimation?
- What can be done to solve the problem of not having planning and estimation?
- How can we make planning and estimation mandatory?

Finding answers to these questions, recording these answers, categorizing them based on the common theme, and analyzing them are the subsequent activities that may be done on the data obtained. These questions can be answered verbally in interviews or considering the limiting factors such as time pressure, large number of respondents, and time zone difference, surveys can be prepared and then sent to the relevant people. The data collection method is explained in the first section of Chapter 2.

Case 2 – Company B has been collecting data related to its annual goals for almost three years. This system was first implemented as part of the preparation for an external appraisal. The collection of data has been continuing during these years, even though the data have not been analyzed since then.

Imagine you are the new manager who was delegated the responsibility to manage the department. What would be your first tasks?

A possible solution is that the new manager sets a meeting with the department and requests a short presentation focusing on these questions:

- Why are the data collected?
- What is the use of data?
- Where can the data be used other than the appraisal?
- How can the data be revised for other purposes?
- Based on the discussions, the manager can make the right decision about data.

Case 3 – Suppose a situation where estimations and actual results vary a lot. What we mean by "a lot" is debatable in terms of management. Therefore, something more comprehensible is needed. The variance exceeds 50 percent in 65 percent of the total cases.

NOTES

Clarity is a paramount issue in management. Try to avoid vague concepts. The attempts made to be clear all the time help with preventing the unnecessary arguments and misunderstandings, which can sometimes lead to critical waste of time and effort.

Considering all the given information, the statement used for describing the situation is as simple as "the variance between estimated and actual results of the time assigned to projects exceeds 50 percent in 65 percent of the total cases." The general characteristic of this situation is what is mostly referred to as "be behind time" in 65 percent of the projects. The specific characteristics of the situation can be extracted by asking such questions:

- How much are we behind the time? Or to put it differently, how much time do we need to catch the plan?
- What were the first estimations, and what is the current measurement?
- What kind of projects are mainly involved in such situations?

- Who or which project manager is/are mainly involved in such situations?
- Which method has been used for estimation?
- Has the estimation method used by other projects? Are they behind the time as well?

These kinds of questions aim at the concepts beyond the surface. They intend to investigate the depth of the problem. "Be behind time" is common to many cases, themes, projects, and sectors. Nonetheless, the investigation of the problem as an individual case with its individual characteristics is the main goal of the second stage of comprehending the current situation, which is investigating the specific characteristics.

Case 4 – You are responsible for completing an online education website project for a customer. The project was scheduled to be delivered in 18 months, and the cost was estimated to be around $350,000. Seven months have passed since the initiation of the project and $160,000 of the total budget was used while the value of the work done is $100,000. How can you describe the situation to a nontechnical simply and to a technical person using the EVA methodology?

Earned Value Analysis (EVA) is a technique used for tracking the project performance. There are many extensions and variations. The main concepts widely used by project managers are:

- Cost Variance (CV) = Estimated value of the work performed (Earned value: EV) – Cost of the work performed (Actual cost: AC)
- Cost Performance Index (CPI) = EV/AC
- Schedule Variance (SV) = EV – Value of work planned (Planned Value: PV) to be performed during a certain period, or cumulative to date
- Schedule Performance Index (SPI) = EV/PV

Let us write the summary of the given information first:

$$\text{Planned time} = 18 \text{ months}$$

$$\text{Estimated cost} = \$350,000$$

$$\text{Time passed} = 7 \text{ months}$$

$$\text{Actual Cost }(\text{AC}) = \$160,000$$

$$\text{Earned Value }(\text{EV}) = \$100,000$$

The calculations are as follow:

$$7/18 \times 100 = 38.88\% \text{ of the planned time}$$

38.88% × \$350,000 = \$136,080 is the planned value (PV) gained based on the planned time and the estimated cost of the project.

$$\text{CV} = \text{EV} - \text{AC} = \$100000 - \$160000 = \$ - 60000$$

$$\text{CPI} = \text{EV}/\text{AC} = 0,625$$

$$\text{SV} = \text{EV} - \text{PV} = \$100,000 - \$136,080 = \$ - 36,080$$

$$\text{SPI} = \text{EV}/\text{PV} = \$100,000/\$136,080 = 0,734$$

Taking a look at the cost variance, it is shown that much more money was spent on the project than the value earned. Thus, the negative CV means that we are in need of extra budget!

CPI is a ratio, and when it is equal to 1, it means that the value earned and what is spent are the same. Any number other than 1 shows a difference between these two values; a CPI ratio greater than one depicts that we gain more than we spend, and on the other hand, a CPI ratio less than 1 implies that we should be more careful about the cost.

SV represents the variance in the schedule between what was planned and what is earned? A negative value is interpreted as being behind the schedule, whereas a positive value demonstrates that the project is ahead of the schedule.

Likewise CPI, SPI is a ratio, and when it equals one, it depicts that the project is exactly going on according to the schedule; a value less than 1 warns that less is done compared with the planned and a value greater than 1 points to the fact that more than what was scheduled is performed.

NOTES

What should always be kept in mind is that numbers are numbers and they don't mean anything or the right thing when they are not analyzed and interpreted well. Similarly, the descriptions and explanations are just words if they are not supported by the data.

What is suggested in this book is not to restrict ourselves to using a sole method or tool, but to give ourselves the opportunity to combine tools and take part or parts from one or several based on our needs. Each project is special, with its very own context, which, for this reason, is required to be taken care of individually.

The explanations earlier should be well examined in the context of the projects, taking into account all the factors involved in order to be able to make the righteous conclusions, make decisions about the solutions, and plan for them.

SWOT Analysis is a strategy tool used for identifying strengths, weaknesses, opportunities, and threats, covering both internal and external analyses. While strengths and weaknesses concentrate on the internal factors, opportunities and threats widen the locus of focus to the environment and market in which the company is located at. The origins of SWOT analysis were investigated in a previous study (Puyt et al., 2023). It was first explained by Alfred Humphrey according to another study (Jain, 2015).

Case 5 – Company C has recently signed a contract for developing an online learning platform for a customer. It will be their first project for a customer from the education sector. The managers have already commenced analyzing their current situation.

What tool, technique, or method would you select if you were one of Company C's managers? SWOT analysis has long been used in diverse fields such as strategic and quality management.

Company C performed the SWOT analysis and the results are shown in the following:

Weakness:

- No previous experiment in the education sector.
- No available resources with education sector-related background.

Strengths:

- Innovative product design and user interface.
- Quick with releasing the product.
- Flexible with customers' change requests due to its agile structure.

As for the external factors, these results were obtained:

Opportunities:

- Opening into new markets by entering the education sector.
- Enhancing our product catalog.
- Leveraging our AI solutions to offer a better user experience.

Threats:

- Entering a new market with new rivals hardly known.
- Risk of our product being imitated soon.

It is worth mentioning that the results of SWOT are the outcome of asking the right and appropriate questions.

Case 6 – Company D has been struggling to balance its activities on different dimensions. It mainly concentrated on innovation and innovative activities after the wide social attention toward AI; nevertheless, it resulted in neglecting their current customers' satisfaction and the survey results depict that their overall customers' satisfaction has dropped drastically compared to the previous years.

What tools, methods, or techniques can be used by Company D to maintain a balanced approach toward various dimensions of a business?

Balanced Score Card was first introduced to help managers view their businesses from four different perspectives, including financial, internal business, customer, and innovation and learning (Kaplan & Norton, 1992). In order to use a balanced scorecard, goals should be first set and measures should be then defined for each perspective.

BSC has been integrated with other tools and models in different contexts. Searching available literature can be of help to decide how to tailor BSC for usage in your case and see its evolution over time.

NOTES

Implementation of models and the use of methods in different contexts are among the subjects of many scientific papers. There are cases where the results gained from the application of tools vary between different contexts. It is a good approach to search for case studies in articles and case books to gain more practical knowledge.

Case 7 – Company E has been requested to prepare a proposal for implementing a health information system in a hospital with sites in different geographical locations. The last time a company released a health information system was two years ago. There are new companies in this field and the environment has changed a lot.

What method can be used to learn more about the possible competitors?

COMPETITOR ANALYSIS

Two stages were defined for the competitor analysis as competitor identification and competitor analysis (Bergena & Peteraf, 2002).

A framework for competitive analysis was suggested embracing two dimensions of market commonality and resource similarity (Chen, 1996).

NOTES

Companies have been implementing various tailored methods for analyzing their competitors. This can be in the form of a list of competitors being assessed in terms of different criteria.

The criteria are the factors important to customers in the choice of the companies they purchase services or products from. It is noteworthy that identification of the criteria is another subject, requiring another procedure. The competitor analysis can be done separately for each product or service.

In Table 1.1, a template for competitor analysis regarding a product is depicted.

Let us take a look at the ways to fill out the cells of this table. There are three choices available here: the quantitative approach, the qualitative approach, or choosing a blended one, which would be less preferable due to its complexity.

Within the quantitative approach, cell A can be completed by taking a number from 1 to 10, implying that competitor 1's product/service takes a number between 1 and 10 considering criterion 1. Likert scale or visuals can be adopted for rating as well.

The qualitative approach requires the user to write comments related to products in terms of criterion 1 in cell A.

Table 1.1 Competitor Analysis for a Product or Service

List of Competitors/Criteria	*Criterion 1*	*Criterion 2*	*Criterion 3*	*Criterion 4*
Competitor 1	A			
Competitor 2				
Competitor 3				

Case 8 – Company F is searching for extra features to be included in their new software. They are not sure about which features to incorporate.

Which method can be beneficial to them in making decisions on the selection of features?

Kano Model is a model introduced in the 1980s (Kano et al., 1984), which brings customer satisfaction into attention in terms of quality, together with considering the functionality.

In order to utilize this model, a structured questionnaire asking the customers to evaluate the attributes of a product/service should be filled out, then analyzed, and finally, the attributes can be categorized.

Quality attributes gained from the Kano model can be classified by making use of other methods. Some of these methods and techniques were reviewed in terms of validity and reliability and are available in the literature (Mikulic´ & Prebezˇac, 2011).

By means of the Kano model, Company F grouped the features as delighters, satisfiers, and dissatisfiers.

NOTES

Methods, tools, and techniques designed evolve over time, and there may be additions, revisions, extensions, or modifications to them. This is the nature of science, evolving! Therefore, a search of the literature may be of great help in making the right decisions, at the right time, and for the right place.

Case 9 – Company G is facing a high degree of turnover rate. New members have joined the teams. In some of the teams, there are problems reported related to the conflicts emerging in the teams.

Stages of Group Development were defined as explaining the stages a group goes through, embracing forming, storming, norming, performing, and adjourning (Tuckman, 1965).

- Do you think the manager should be worried about the disputes and disagreements that occur as a result of having new members attending their teams?
- What are the reasons behind the commitment of some employees and the noncommitment of the others?

Storming is the stage at which conflicts arise within the team.

The second question tackles the concept of commitment and its antecedents. Organizational commitment has been the subject of myriads of studies in the field of organizational behavior. Similarly, human resources practitioners have paid great attention to it, specifically in the sectors where the turnover rate is naturally high like the IT sector. As it can be comprehended, increasing the organizational commitment is related to the turnover rate negatively. Let us take a quick look at the results of some of the recent relevant studies:

- The results of one of the studies conducted on employees in the tourism and hospitality sectors have depicted that commitment and turnover intention of employees are moderately and negatively correlated (Guzeller & Celiker, 2019).
- In another interesting research, compensation was also considered in the conceptual model together with organizational commitment and turnover intention, where data were collected from the health sector. The findings pointed to the negative relationship between compensation and turnover intention while showing that compensation influences organizational commitment positively and concluded that good organizational commitment decreases the turnover intention (Silaban & Syah, 2018).

Organizational Commitment was conceptualized as consisting of three components affective, normative, and continuance and was defined as a psychological state associated with the relationship between the employee and the organization that influences the decision of staying with or leaving the organization (Meyer & Allen, 1991).

NOTES

In practice, there might not be a clear line between some of the duties of an agile coach or project manager, a human resource expert, and a workplace psychologist!

There come the situations where you need to motivate your team members and keep up their spirits like a psychologist; when you need to listen to your team members about their dissatisfaction with the compensation and communicate with the human resources department to avoid their resignation; when you stand up for your team and share their requests with the top management; when you need to appreciate the difficult situation a team member of yours has experienced and soothe the stress with your words. Even if they may seem somehow unprofessional or out of the scope of your duty, such cases will be encountered, and we need to learn how to handle them.

Case 10 – Company H has decided to develop a guide for managing its different projects in order to standardize the execution of the project management practices within the company. It is noteworthy that all the project managers hold international certificates in project management and the company allocates an annual budget to purchase the updated trainings and certificates and also to renew them.

They are searching for ways to classify their projects.

What do you recommend them to do?

There are many ways to categorize projects and numerous factors to consider while performing the classification. The factor that is usually noticed by the project managers in the first place is complexity. There are tools available to measure the complexity of the projects, and based on the calculated value, the guides are present to navigate different levels of complexity.

NTCP (Novelty, Technology, Complexity, and Pace) Model was first developed by taking the three dimensions of uncertainty, complexity, and pace to characterize projects, and then uncertainty was divided based on its two main sources: market and technological (Shenhar & Dov, 2007).

The alternative but a time-consuming way is to prepare a classification guide by asking the project managers about the factors bearing significance in grouping and then making a list, refining it, and finalizing it.

Having a glance at the literature also provides you with many valuable options.

This model not only helps with the categorization of the projects but also provides a tool for comparing between required and actual styles of project management and assisting the managers on decisions about the benefits and risks of the projects (Shenhar & Dov, 2007).

What about the situation in which we have a portfolio of projects?

NOTES

There are terms that are incorrectly used interchangeably. Sometimes, the words are perceived differently by different individuals and no one asks for a clarification because he/she thinks that might seem unknowledgeable. For instance, once a friend of mine who had newly joined a company asked for the long form of an acronym widely used in meetings. What happened next might surprise you. The user and the participants in the meeting could not come up with a common definition for the acronym! Everyone explained a distinct phrase for the acronym! For this reason, as a recommendation for the companies, there should be a "glossary" prepared for each company encompassing the words and terms related to that specific sector along with the words and terms that are specific to that company. The benefits of such a glossary include but are not limited to:

- *Avoiding probable misunderstandings.*
- *Helping the new joiners to adapt sooner to the usage of words and terms.*
- *Providing a standardization in terms of terminology.*

Moving back to the question, what are the definitions of project, program, and portfolio? Let us draw your attention to Figure 1.2.

Program is a group of relevant projects, and similarly, the portfolio is a group of related projects and programs. In projects, the efforts of the project manager are with the aim to provide the deliverables of the project while trying to control for the scope, budget, and time.

Program managers coordinate the projects in the program, allocate and balance the resources across them, while at the portfolio level, we can talk of strategy! Management of portfolios involves ensuring that the business achieves the strategic values and reaches its strategic objectives.

Returning to the question of how to classify portfolios of projects in software companies, we may take a look at the literature.

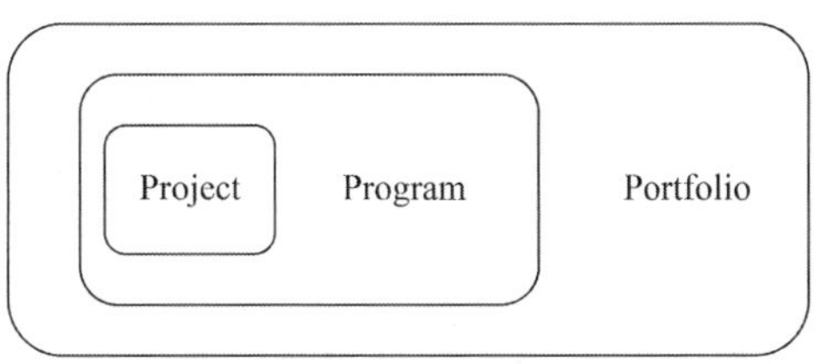

Figure 1.2 Project, program, and portfolio.

Portfolio Selection is about making the right choice about the projects to be included in the portfolio either selected from current projects or project proposals. The critical issue is to form the portfolio in a way that it achieves the objectives of the company while not going beyond the resources available or stretching the constraints (Archer & Ghasemzadeh, 1999).

Project Portfolio Selection Framework was proposed, including the following "major stages": pre-screening, individual project analysis, screening, optimal portfolio selection, and portfolio adjustment, with each stage having an objective and being succeeded by the next stage (Archer & Ghasemzadeh, 1999).

Sometimes there is a need to ask for ideas of different people while taking into consideration not one, but more than a criterion similar to the research conducted on the portfolio selection of software development projects by using the analytical hierarchy process (AHP) in software companies (Kaiser et al., 2019).

Another study made suggestions for building a good project portfolio of which some of them are: forming the team with experienced individuals, implementing agile methodology where possible, avoiding unneeded changes within the team, gaining knowledge from the lessons learned, and executing portfolio strategy for medium and long terms (Huijgens et al., 2014).

Case 11 – Company I wants to allocate the projects among project managers. They have held several meetings and the points at which they reached can be summarized as follows:

- The director can allocate the projects to the project managers subjectively as it was done before.
- A guide can be prepared for project allocation to standardize the procedure for the prevention of subjective decision-making.
- There are many criteria that make it hard to decide on which to include and exclude in decision-making.

How would you help the company I with their decision-making process?

What comes to mind at first glance is that no one wants a subjective process. Everyone seeks some kind of logical justification behind each decision made.

Organizational Justice can be described by considering two types of subjective perceptions: being fair in allocating the outcomes and being fair in the decision concerning the allocation of outcomes (Colquitt et al., 2001).

In the same article, three types of organizational justice are explained: distributive, procedural, and interactional, of which the last, itself, has two types of interpersonal justice and informational justice (Colquitt et al., 2001).

NOTES

Knowing different concepts of organizational behavior can help managers understand the reasons for the existence and demonstration of behavior in a company. We all have encountered managers who have responded to our questions regarding the procedures taken to reach a decision such as "accept it as it is or quit!" Be sure that your question was not awkward one or even abnormal.

Many software companies have identified the need for their managers to know the management concepts. This originates from the fact that most managers of software companies are coming from technical people, software engineers, and software experts who, after years of experience and hardworking, have reached their current positions. Organizing management-related trainings and webinars with topics such as "how to lead your team," "leadership skills," "empowering your teams," and many other alternatives can equip them with the insight and knowledge to develop their managing skills.

The number of project managers who believe that tough projects are always assigned to them is not low! Although some may feel proud to manage these kinds of projects, it can be a cause of burnout and resignation in the long term. Besides, the risk of failure for projects with more complexity level is higher than the other projects, which puts the project manager in a position prone to failing.

All the aforementioned information highlights the need for implementing an objective decision-making system in a company.

What can we do with the criteria? Which can be left out?

Whenever we are talking of several criteria, multiple criteria decision-making methods and techniques can be utilized.

Multi-Criteria Decision Making (MCDM) or **Multi-Criteria Decision Analysis (MCDA)** entails various methods used for making decisions taking several criteria into account.

Many tools have been developed using these methods, which facilitate manual calculations. For instance, the tool asks the user about criteria, their weights, and the available options and shows the prioritized list of the options on the final screen.

Employing MCDM methods in diverse contexts has been the subject of many studies. Interestingly, the use of these methods has not been specific to academic works. Many companies have gained benefits from these methods in developing their mobile applications like route optimization and software applications for different purposes, such as performance management.

NOTES

Sometimes, preparing procedures is deemed as the waste of time and drudgery work. Many quality-related tasks deal with preparing some kind of documentation. Despite the tremendous effort that rests behind them, these tasks are implied as trivial. Some of the benefits of having comprehensive documentation are:

- *Making objective decisions based on predefined procedures.*
- *Affecting procedural organizational justice positively.*
- *Taking the role of a guide for new joiners.*
- *Providing legal protection.*
- *Sharing information and improving communication.*
- *Having transparency in the procedures.*

Maintaining consistency in the execution of policies and procedures.

Case 12 – Managers and directors of Company J have been holding meetings about improving their processes. During these meetings, process excellence, business process management (BMP), capability maturity models (CMM), and standards have been discussed. The variety of choices has made the situation even more complex, and they are not sure how to proceed. These questions were raised:

- Should we purchase business process tools?
- Should we employ a process manager?
- Should we hire an external consultant for models and standards?
- Should we educate our current staff on the subjects?
- Should an already experienced manager be designated as the process manager?

We may review the literature concerning these concepts.

Business Process Management (BPM) roots back to the concept of Process Reengineering (BPR) management (Grisold et al., 2022). It consists of principles and tools to help organizations achieve their business objectives through improving their processes.

Five principles of BPM are: pervasiveness, ownership, documentation, measurement, and inspection (Lee & Dale, 1998).

In a similar vein, rules have been suggested for developing a BMP culture, and some of them can be briefly explained this way:

- As a systematic methodology, it is a way for continuous improvement for providing high-quality products and services.
- Process management is considered the way to excellence, which aims to enhance activities by introducing best practices to keep internal performance standards at a competitively acceptable level.
- Through continuous measurement and improvement, BPM assures the effectiveness of the process (Zairi, 1997).

BPM can be either explorative or exploitative where the former is proactive in reengineering new processes whereas the latter is about improving current processes (Grisold et al., 2022).

Let us move a bit further in time and see what BPR means.

Business Process Reengineering (BPR) was used for pointing at the role of process management in creating competitive advantage in the 1990s (O'Neill & Sohal, 1999).

What rests at the core of reengineering in discontinuous thinking, which happens through breaking the old rules and assumptions on the basis of operations and questioning them (Hammer, 1990).

NOTES

Business process engineering has attracted the attention of many practitioners during decades. There was a period during which any attempts toward improving the processes were labeled as "reengineering" for the purpose of demonstrating the work done, excessively fruitful, and revolutionary. As the time passed, the concept took its right place in the market and the practices were much more aligned with the theory and the righteous applications.

Taking a walk through the practice and what is happening out in the field shows that the design of the processes has gained much more significant attention during recent years compared to the past. Many companies have already begun to allocate remarkable and distinct budgets to process improvement activities. It is only lately that we can come across positions such as process improvement expert, process manager, quality improvement manager, operational excellence expert, and process excellence manager in job listings and on recruitment websites.

Before, process improvement used to be perceived as a kind of luxury for firms, being regarded as an extra workload to the employees, and as it can be comprehended, there was not much time left for process improvement in its real terms! We should not underestimate the great efforts and extraordinary diligence of the companies that have brought up invaluable insights and solutions for making the processes work more effectively and efficiently during decades.

This, again, reminds of the importance of having the theory and practice, go ahead hand in hand.

Cost-Benefit Analysis is a decision support method by which the benefits and costs related to an option are listed, and then they are analyzed to see which one outweighs the others.

Supplier Selection Criteria have been grouped in different ways. Five selection criteria identified by researchers are: integrative, adaptive, performance, economic, and legalistic, which can be put in other words, excluding legalistic aspects such as: service, delivery, quality, and price (Wilson, 1994).

Returning to the first question regarding a tool purchase, the following method could be beneficial for our decision-making.

Cost-benefit analysis can be combined with MCDM methods (mentioned earlier in this chapter) where numerous criteria are involved. To put it differently, is the price the only criterion a company takes into account when evaluating the suppliers? Of course not in most cases! We may elaborate on this issue with a simple example. You are searching for an Internet Service Provider (ISP), and your research ends up with a list of seven companies. How do you make a choice? Do you just go on with the cheapest alternative even though deciding on the cheapest option might not be that easy in some situations?

NOTES

Many companies have their own criteria tailored based on their needs, although almost the very common criteria still rest are: service, delivery, quality, and price.

Additionally, lots of companies have begun to request specific certifications from their suppliers. Thus, possessing specific certifications can be regarded as a criterion in the selection process. This has become even more important in software companies. Apart from the competition that compels the companies to incorporate the practices of standards and/or models, certifications are sometimes held as a pre-requirement for participating in tenders. Furthermore, taking the growing number of startups and companies active in the IT sector, certifications, badges, medals, awards, or any kind of endorsement from an external party, especially reputable and well-known entities, play a vital part in surpassing competitors.

Moreover, it is worth mentioning that the day-by-day increasing inclination toward sustainable products has already made its impact on the decisions made by the customers with regard to their product or service supplier. Gradually, sustainability initiatives are taking their place among the criteria for the selection of suppliers. Sustainability encompasses a broad term of activities associated with social, environmental, and governance dimensions. The criteria can be broken down into these dimensions as well.

During making purchasing decisions, it's crucial to look beyond the initial cost.

Total Cost of Ownership (TCO) is a tool that enables users to understand the true cost of a product or a service from a particular supplier (Ellram, 1995).

TCO can be used for supplier evaluation and selection and is a great tool for analyzing the transaction costs associated with the supplier (Ellram, 1995), taking into account all costs contrary to price-only approaches, which only deem the price as the basis for supplier selection.

When talking of transaction cost, two paramount concepts in strategic management are better to be discussed: transaction cost theory and agency theory.

Transaction Cost Theory (TCT) regards a company and the market organization as different modes of governance of which the prominent three are: market, hierarchies, and hybrids; besides, according to this theory, adaptation is the main issue a company faces, and the main goal pursued by an organization is to reduce the expenditure (Williamson, 2014).

Agency Theory describes the relation between two sides: the principal and the agent, where the principal is a person or persons delegating tasks to the agent to do on his/her behalf (Jensen & Meckling, 1976).

This theory is simply about the fact that when a principal or principals give a job to the agent to perform it, the agents' interest might vary from the principal's, and there, the agency costs can be defined.

One of the most difficult decisions in software companies is information technology outsourcing. There are conditions where software companies prefer to buy an IT service from an external supplier instead of allocating time and budget to make it on their own, even if they have the ability to produce it. To say it in a clearer way, software companies provide software to their customers, and they, themselves, are customers of other IT companies.

Information Technology Outsourcing, defined as the transmission of a company's IT-relevant operations to an external body, commenced in the 1990s to complement in-house IT efforts of the companies and has been continuing since then (Pati & Desai, 2005).

NOTES

When you first start working at a software company, you encounter many occasions at which you ask yourself, "why doesn't the company develop this software itself?," "why cannot it assign a team to develop this tool?"

After some time, you began to understand that the software industry is not just about writing a working code! The tool should be responsible, reliable, and available and bear many other characteristics, while it needs to be maintained and updated from time to time. You send an email when the tool is not working or create a ticket on their customer relationship management platform. Imagine the tool was made by your company. Would it be that easy? Of course not.

Put all these aside, you will have an environment full of programmers, start-ups, and ready-to-go-start-ups, all who can imitate your product and come up with more functional, innovative, or user-friendly alternatives in as short as a few days. Are you ready to compete for survival?

Pati and Desai (2005) have proposed a conceptual model helping with the comprehension of these relationships: an organization assesses its internal capabilities concerning an IT service opportunity and the potential strategic business value that could be derived from it, and the results of this assessment have an impact on the decision, whether to outsource the service or keep it in-house (Pati & Desai, 2005).

Outsourcing is not a simple strategic choice. It can be viewed from many perspectives, like TCT, competitive advantage, and agency theory.

TCT and agency theory proposed four risks related to outsourcing, which are: getting involved in a lock-in relationship; bearing the costs of changes to the contract; having unforeseen costs raised, including both transaction and management costs; and disagreements and legal acts (Bahli & Rivard, 2003).

The next subject related to **Case 12** is about choosing whether to continue the process with the resources within the company or to apply for external resources. Various opinions and standpoints are available on this topic:

- Some encourage companies to stick to their internal resources for many reasons of which the most prominent one is to minimize and eliminate the risk of dependency on external entities.
- The other studies defend the utilization of external resources and back their ideas with reasons such as: obtaining the opportunity to work with experienced people; bringing new and innovative ideas into the company; making the working environment more competitive as the employees may feel internally obliged to develop and update their skills and knowledge; and capitalizing on the knowledge and experience of the experts who the company cannot afford to hire full-time.
- The remainder of the studies recommend companies to leverage both external and internal resources; the external resources bear the advantage of seeing the problems outside of the border of a company

and performing benchmarking as they have the flexibility to work with different companies.

- On the other hand, the internal resources are wholly familiar with the dynamics going on inside a company and are able to screen the best set of choices fitted with the company's context. The noteworthy issue is that the risk of path dependency in the decisions and actions of these individuals can be mitigated in the presence of external resources.

NOTES

Let us leverage the concepts mentioned so far to interpret the situation of Company J.

If Company J is to select using external resources, it should carefully examine issues such as:

- *How can we select among different suppliers?*
- *How can the relationship with the agent be managed?*
- *How can we monitor the agent?*
- *How much will it cost for us to work with an agent?*
- *Is it cost-beneficial to us to buy the service?*
- *What will be the risks to appoint an agent?*

Having a glance at the practice, some other notions can fit here as well.

The day-by-day increasing concern regarding notions of privacy and information security has created an extra pain point for companies when it comes to supplier selection. The main questions are what information can be shared, to what extent, and in which form. These have had a great impact on us as users as well. We, just like the companies, think twice before picking a supplier for a service or product since we are expected to share some of our personal information with them. You may remember when it first became common to be asked for your name, phone number, and email, and how you might have tried to skip providing them. Now, we are sharing more information and we are not even aware or care as much as before! With all that mentioned, the importance of auditing your company's IT suppliers for privacy and information security can be well apprehended.

The other matter that would have an impact on your company's relationship with your supplier is the sustainability-related audit. The growing focus and the heightened awareness toward sustainability have brought new challenges to the supplier relationship. More companies are now expected to conduct audits on their suppliers with regard to human rights practices, labor rights initiatives, and their environmental impact. It raises the questions of: who will be responsible for these kinds of audits; when will they be conducted; how will they be conducted (on-site or off-site); according to which standard or framework will the supplier be audited; what should the results like to be considered satisfactory; what if the requirements are not met; and so on.

To conclude, determining the external resource usage necessitates the careful examination of all these points and planning for cost, time, and scope.

Talking of resources, some concepts may need more clarification here.

Resource-Based View (RBV) leverages the capabilities and resources within a company to create a competitive advantage, which affects the strategic choices that the company made (Madhani, 2009).

It is noteworthy that not all resources can be viewed as a source of competitive advantage. In the presence of the conditions of resource heterogeneity and resource immobility, competitive advantage emerges (Madhani, 2009).

RBV speaks of both resources and capabilities. To make them clearer, resources are assets that a company controls, while capabilities are a group of resources that enable benefiting wholly from the other resources (Barney & Hesterly, 2008).

Competitive Advantage (CA) as comprehended from its name is the advantage a company can obtain, enabling it to outperform its rivals and hold a superior position in the market.

Barney (1991) defined CA as executing a strategy that creates value while it is not implemented by any other competitors at the same time. It turns into a sustained CA when other companies are not able to reproduce the advantages of that strategy (Barney, 1991).

The resources, if bearing specific characteristics, will become a CA to the company.

VRIN are the initials of the four attributes for a resource to become sustained competitive advantage as valuable, rare, inimitable, and nonsubstitutability (Barney, 1991).

VRIO represents concepts of value, rarity, inimitability, and organization, through which the potential of a resource or capability to become a CA is investigated (Barney & Hesterly, 2008).

The distinction between two notions can be made by deeming their main points; VRIN concentrates on the resource level while VRIO takes the functionality and/or utility of the resource into account, nevertheless, the level of analysis is a resource in both (Cardeal & António, 2012).

Obtaining CA which was traditionally believed to be possible through strategic, financial, and technological capabilities, require the individuals of an organization to be committed as well, which makes the organizational capability the fourth source of CA (Ulrich & Lake, 1991).

Organizational Capability is the employee management ability of the company with the aim of achieving CA; it is not necessarily about employing the best individuals, but the competent ones, and cultivating their skills (Ulrich & Lake, 1991).

NOTES

The fact is that you may have the best crew on the board but are still struggling to outperform the competitors!

Managing an organization is like conducting an orchestra. You should have good players, and you should make the synergy happen within the team. As good players do not mean good music if they are not aligned and coordinated well, a company full of talents will not yield the desired results if not managed effectively and efficiently.

In recent years, especially, software companies have directed their ways toward the enhancement of their talent management programs. They have widened their scope from recruiting the best to maintaining the best performers and creating the best through on-the-job training and skill development. Participating actively in career fairs, looking for new benefits that can be provided to the employees, defining different types of paid leaves like birthday leave, offering employees discounts for services or products, executing an open-door policy, and preferring agile approaches rather than the traditional ones to motivate and empower employees are just part of their endeavor to affect the organizational performance positively.

Talent Management was assigned seven core functions, conceptualized and named in a recent paper, which can be summarized as: formulating the talent-related plans, identifying the talented individuals, gaining the attention of them, hiring them, developing the talent, followed by deploying and retaining them (Yildiz & Esmer, 2023).

NOTES

There is another topic that is brought up a lot in the meetings by human resources and top management. You may have heard the sentence "keep your team engaged!"

At first glance, it seems like another interchangeable word for commitment or something related to it. You may be right as its positive relationship with organizational commitment has been proven in several studies. Although they are two distinct concepts.

Work Engagement was explained as considering your job as a source of your energy where you are willing to give more to it and you intend to focus completely on it (Yalabik et al., 2015).

On-the-Job Training is preferred by companies for three main reasons: training costs and benefits, just-in-time training approach, and the reflection of the learned concepts in the situation of work of the employee (Van der Klink & Streumer, 2002).

NOTES

The effectiveness of the on-the-job training and the results can be searched by delving into the literature on this topic; however, the noteworthy matter is measuring the effectiveness of any kind of training presented to the employees.

Measurement is non-negotiable in quality management and, in particular, in organizational training. Quality departments, in collaboration with the human resources department, hold the main responsibility for identifying the training needs of the individuals and arranging the training in many companies. What is seen in practice is that the trainings are provided, and at the end of the trainings, a survey is sent to the participants to learn about their satisfaction level and the weaknesses and strengths they identify within the training. And, then, it is all counted as finished. Even the metrics used are limited to the percentage of employees who received training and not more. Checking on the effectiveness of training is easily overlooked or intentionally neglected due to many possible reasons of which the main is not knowing how to measure their effectiveness. The first option is organizing an exam from the content of the training, but you surely have seen how they are performed; asking your colleagues to take the tests instead of you; searching for the answers on the search engines; or using AI chatbots. What managers and specifically top managers want to see is not a point nor a certificate, but how the changes in your skills and/or knowledge rooting from training are reflected in your job, which goes far beyond the surface.

Test scores of the tests held after training were labeled as "declarative knowledge" and to take a step further, a multi-dimensional view was depicted for the effectiveness of training, consisting of the aforementioned dimension along with training transfer, training maintenance, and training generalization (Chiaburu & Tekleab, 2005).

Looking at the concepts from a strategic point of view posits a lot of importance on the human resources and encourages the employers to make them a source of competitive advantage.

Resource-Dependency Theory was formed around the idea that an organization is potentially dependent on its external resources in terms of physical and financial resources and the information that is provided by the environment (Pfeffer & Salancik, 2003).

The other notion that is related to resources and can be confused with a resource-based view is resource-dependency theory, despite the fact that they uphold different viewpoints.

As we all know, companies are not working in isolation, and they are in connection with their environment, encompassing their rivals, customers, and resources, and from a system viewpoint, they exchange information and resources with it.

NOTES

A very distinguishing characteristic of studies related to organizations is that decisions cannot be made taking the internal dynamics and factors solely into account. Organizations are affected by their environments to various extents. Let us illuminate this with an example.

Employees of a company are in need for more comprehensive online banking solutions. They are needed to go to their banks from time to time, and this results in constant hourly leaves. They came up with the solution for the bank by using technologies such as voice and facial recognition to avoid these unnecessary visits. If they only focus on their needs and the internal dynamics, their solution is warmly welcomed. But what about the solutions offered by their rivals? What about what is going on out in the market?

Since there are already similar solutions for online banking, these questions raise:

- *Does the bank ignore or delay transformation?*
- *Why doesn't the bank choose these solutions?*
- *How is the proposed solution different from other available ones?*

Imagine we initiate the project and deliver the solution to the bank. We might have obtained benefits, but how long does it last? Isn't our customer highly willing to switch to new solutions as ours is not competent?

Managers and top managers know that keeping a customer satisfied is much more effort-taking than winning a new customer since it was proved to be more cost beneficial too. No pain, no gain! Your royal customers' conversations with their friends and colleagues and their posts on social media are your best advertisements, which do not require an extra allocated budget.

In conclusion, if the environment is taken lightly, the customers' needs might not be comprehended well; the competitors will not be analyzed thoroughly; the resources will be lacked and not provided; and how can a company survive without the presence and provision of sufficient resources and customers?

The impact of the environment has also led to the formation of diverse economic agglomerations, particularly in the IT sector.

Clusters are varieties of economic agglomerations.

Clusters were defined as the gatherings of companies from the same industry geographically in order to reach various benefits (Fidanboy, 2022).

The specific characteristics of the IT sector, particularly the need for resources, allow the formation of IT clusters, which are a type of technology clusters (Boja, 2011). The same paper outlines the approaches a company from a cluster can take to become competitive, such as becoming the first implementer of innovative technologies and becoming the leader of a segment of the market by means of continuous innovation (Boja, 2011). A more relevant recent concept is the digital industrial cluster.

Digital Industrial Cluster (DIC) has been newly proposed as a virtual space where companies can gain benefits of the technological infrastructures expected to back their digitally transformable organizational functions, which at last eases digitalization (Fernandez-Escobedo et al., 2024).

NOTES

Innovation can be categorized into different groups, but what we usually prefer is to label it as either radical or incremental innovation.

Software companies mostly focus on incremental innovation, where they add different features and make improvements to their existing products and services, either theirs or others.

Radical innovation, even if rarely seen, can have a great impact on the market. We can illustrate it as infusing some kind of tendency into the environment: the tendency to imitate the innovative idea or the intention to come up with an innovation exceeding the previous.

Software companies have formulated a variety of strategies to foster radical innovations, like organizing hackathons and competitions. An invaluable statement that a member of a hackathon jury once mentioned was: "there are myriads of ideas, a few are feasible, and a fewer to execute them!" This may shed light on the fact why so many start-ups fail. Having an idea is not practically sufficient. There should be a feasible way to implement it, and there exists the need for a person or persons to bring it into reality. How we express it in simple words while we are guiding our teams is: There should be Cindarella (dreamer or innovator), pumpkins (physical resources), and Fairy Grandmother (the doer or the executor who is capable of making the dream come true). The right timing should not be disregarded since it is the key to defeat the rivals. And besides, leveraging an idea is time bounded. A new technology is no more new and appealing when the newer ones are introduced to the market or it will be no longer profitable when the alternatives are launched with a more reasonable price, a better design, or an extra feature.

If it can be put this way, there exists much tougher theory regarding the effects of the environment on the companies: selection of who survives or who fails.

Population Ecology attempts to bring the locus of focus from the organization itself of its environment; a shift from the internal view to the external view of the organization; a transition from the adaptation approach to the selection approach.

It expresses how environmental variations together with competition can shape the population of the organizations and have an impact on their growth rates (Hannan & Freeman, 1989).

Resource dependency theory and population ecology both focus on the environment when trying to understand organizations. The main differences between these two theories were explained as the following:

- The emphasis of the population ecology is on the selection, while the resource dependency theory stresses adaptation.
- According to the population ecology, the main reasons behind the changes in the population are the emergence and elimination of organizations in the population, and it does not elaborate on the internal organizational dynamics (Pfeffer & Salancik, 2003).

Case 13 – Company K has passed a year full of changes to their goals and strategies. The fact is that they were not able to reach their annual goals, and to cover their failure, they altered their goals and targets instead. They are now planning to formulate new strategies for the upcoming year, and from what they have learned, they must define their strategies much more realistically compared to the last year.

How can you guide them through their strategy formation process?

How can you identify a good strategy?

The details in relation to the notion of strategy are covered in Chapter 3. As for this case, we may look at the attributes of a good strategy.

A Good Strategy may have various characteristics and can be defined in different manners. Some of the common characteristics suggested by a study are:

- Being clear,
- Being objective,
- Setting simple goals,
- A thorough knowledge and apprehension of the competitive environment,
- Comprehending and utilizing the resources objectively,
- Implementing an effective plan (Enríquez-De-La-O, 2015).

NOTES

Observing and reviewing the execution of the strategies in software companies shed light on these common problems, which are either directly or indirectly associated with the characteristics described earlier.

Sometimes, strategies are not clarified well due to a main reason, which is: the policymakers or strategists do not have a clear vision of the strategies, and as a result, they are not able to illustrate it thoroughly. This inability originates from them knowing the situation superficially, or that might be due to their preference, which they considered wise. You may ask how. They leave the interpretation of the strategies to their executors, with the intention of having the strategy executors perceive them as they find appropriate for their context. They believe that this may reduce the risks by giving the executor the chance of incorporating the relevant contextual factors into decision-making. Nonetheless, the risk of going astray from the organizational objectives can become a bigger problem when the right decisions are not made, and subsequently, the suitable activities are not planned, and what is reached is not what is meant to be.

Objectivity! What we appraise most in decision-making is objectivity! Subjectivities bring about many negative effects to companies. This is not only of importance in the strategy formation process. Even in the evaluation of the progress toward the objectives, the 10 one takes and the 10 the other takes should be almost entirely objective and all the procedures and processes relating to the outcome should be explained in detail. Unfortunately, we pinpoint this problem in many software companies. The progress is measured subjectively despite using the metrics and measures. The main reason is that regardless of having the quantitative data, the interpretation remains dependent on the manager or who is in charge.

Given all mentioned, quality experts' assistance is needed in strategy making, and they should make attempts to standardize the metrics and measures for the objectives. Additionally, they can contribute to the overall strategy by preparing written procedure and communicating it to the employees, and providing guidance to the evaluators.

Simple goals or simply worded goals are not usually welcomed by companies, particularly for those companies that are the leaders in their sector. They think that complex wording seems more professional and advanced. Let us give you an example. A company may set its financial goal as: "increasing financial performance by 20%" or it can be worded as "optimizing financial performance by employing a multifaceted and comprehensive approach, aiming to realize a 20 percent *enhancement in our overall financial outcomes." Thus, the key is here: "keep it simple and understandable!" By doing so, vagueness and confusion will be minimized. One of the practical solutions companies implement is holding workshops with their c-levels or/and all of those who will be in charge of executing strategies. This facilitates the correct interpretation and, consequently, the correct devising of plans.*

Competition and strategy are intertwined notions. Strategic making and strategic management cannot be conducted without taking the competition into account. Understanding the rivals and the methods available are reviewed in detail in Chapter 3.

Another issue which we, as consultants, have detected in the software companies is the misallocation of the resources; the strategies are set, despite the fact that there are not enough resources to realize them, and after some time, or at the end of the year, the strategies are terminated.

The other problematic situation is that execution of strategies is overloaded to a team or department, and the other teams are much more free in terms of the strategies assigned to them.

The last common issue is inappropriate allocation; wrong people at their wrong places. The strategies should detect the resources that have the capability of becoming a competitive advantage to the company. You may have heard or watched the videos of successful strategists who say; "I sensed that he/she was the right choice." When the subject turns from characteristics of a good strategy to characteristics of a good strategist, knowing your people and their capabilities is an incontrovertible and undeniable attribute.

As important as the strategy formation is the planning and execution of strategies. In this scope, the role of governance should not be underestimated, and for this reason, a good governance structure should be portrayed.

It is noteworthy that there are many software companies that have employed digital tools to track their progress toward the strategies. Nevertheless, AI-enabled tools, business intelligence tools, and whatever solutions are employed should be accompanied with accurate perception, interpretation, and action plans of the strategy makers.

In relation to strategies and decisions, an interesting subject concerning the consistency of the new decisions with the past ones is path dependency. It is easily overlooked by the managers.

Path-Dependency in decision-making and strategy setting occurs when they are being affected by the past. These factors may be the previous decisions, expectations, fears, and hopes (Gáspár, 2011).

NOTES

Failure of many companies is caused not by an inaccurate strategy but a train of them. The previous decisions may have an impact on our future decisions. This is mainly due to the belief that if our decision at time t1 is this, our decision at time t2 should be that in order for the strategies to be effective and that is the trap of being locked-in in a situation.

The tip is to be ready for any kind of change. You should be able to predict some part of changes to an extent, however, unpredictable changes are inevitable, and you should have plans regarding how to handle such cases, a generic plan.

Quality experts can help strategists to develop such plans, which is extremely useful in change management and risk management.

NOTES

You may have heard the sentence of "new blood is required on the team." Myriads of reasons might rest behind this decision of which the most common ones are:

- *Need for new insights and ideas coming from outside; it is just like asking someone to see a specific problem from another angel, which is an effective way to examine diverse aspects of a situation and learn about various viewpoints.*

- *Need for more revolutionary opinions contrary to the thoughts of the ones on the team, which have been affected by the same factors for a long time.*
- *Preventing any locked-in situation in decisions; members of the team know what the others might think of their ideas, therefore, some thoughts will not be revealed at all; old team members have experience and knowledge of what previous decisions lead to, thus, they would not welcome the ones that might believe end same!; and the team members might have been so drowned in their routines that thinking of another option and stepping outside of their comfort zone may seem almost unachievable.*

The newcomer should be given the chance to come up with his thoughts without harsh objections. He/she should be encouraged to share his/her opinions. Nonetheless, unfortunately, he/she is highly probable to be ceased after some time by the older members of the team and accused of:

- *Not knowing the dynamics of the situations,*
- *And/or he/she has no idea of how decisions work in the company,*
- *Or he/she is not familiar enough with the internal interactions.*

The mediating role here is part of the management responsibility to foster the flow of new ideas, otherwise, the new will be faded, and the old will be dressed in new, which, deep in nature, will not be fruitful in the long term.

The relationship between path dependency and path creation was depicted in Gaspar's paper (2011): path dependency describes how the past influences the present and future, whereas path creation is about the future vision having an impact on the present and past.

Path Creation, in contrast to path dependency, involves a concept of agency that is both distributed and emergent, arising through relational processes that shape and define phenomena (Gáspár, 2011).

In path creation, rather than focusing on repeating or sidestepping past occurrences, actors draw on history to develop new options and plan new initiatives and strategies for the future (Garud et al., 2010).

Taking path creation into consideration, as for Case 13, Company K needs to have a meeting, probably a retrospective meeting, to extract the following three information and record them for further examination and investigation:

- What went well?
- What could have been done better?, which represents the improvement areas.
- What should not have been repeated again?

Seeking the answers to the earlier questions and preparing a list of lessons learned can be of great help to Company K in formulating the strategies for the following year. Furthermore, benchmarking and competitor analysis can also be performed to align our strategies with the external environment.

We mentioned external factors. Are there any methods to inspect the external factors in a neat way?

PESTEL is a method for depicting the situation of a company in its environment at the macro level. Two main functions were stated for it: examination of the environment a company is active in and provision of information for foreseeing the situation might emerge in the future (Yüksel, 2012).

The same paper employed PESTEL as a representative of these dimensions: political, economic, socio-cultural, technological, environment, and legal (Yüksel, 2012).

NOTES

When it comes to practice, companies have their own way of utilizing the tools. PESTEL analysis provides a high-level image of the environment to the company, which is not practically of use to all managers but to those who have responsibility in drawing the path for the company, together with the strategists.

The list can be prepared either horizontally or vertically or even in a circular form, and similarly, some dimensions can be eliminated based on the needs and context, in line with the research conducted so far.

The first noteworthy subject here is the day-by-day increasing attention toward environment topics as sustainability gains popularity and becomes a mandate rather than a preference.

Table 1.2 A Tailored PESTEL Analysis

	Dimensions/ Weight (1 to 10)	*P(5)*	*E(6)*	*S(9)*	*T(10)*	*E(7)*	*L(9)*
Factor (Opportunity or Threat/ Weight)		Factor 1(O/5)					
		Factor 2(T/1)					
		Factor 3(O/2)					
		Factor 4(T/1)					
Total Weight of Each Dimension		45					

The second issue is that PESTEL can be integrated with MCDM tools for the purpose of illustrating a much more detailed picture. The very simple application can be using criteria and weight assignment when listing factors.

A tailored PESTEL analysis example is shown in Table 1.2. Factors detected can either have a positive impact on the company featuring as an opportunity or may bear negative effects on the company, representing threats.

Case 14 – Company L has decided to direct all its objectives toward increasing productivity.

- Where should they begin from?
- What do they mean by productivity?
- To what extent do they want to increase productivity? Is there a qualitative target? If yes, is the qualitative target the same for all the departments or does it vary among them?
- Is productivity the same as efficiency?

Productivity Growth was defined as the total change in the output as a result of change in efficiency together with technical change where efficiency is about the variance between a case and the cutting edge of technology (Grosskopf, 1993).

Productivity is dependent on how companies compete with each other, and it does not rely on the areas they are in competition within (Porter, 1998).

NOTES

Looking at the definition provided, what can be understood is that productivity is related to the environment of a company, more specifically to its competitors. Having an extra eye for your competitors is not an option but a mandate!

The other issue is that increasing productivity is usually set as a goal for a company and it is cascaded to the operational units. The main problem that we usually observe in the companies is that no data is available to show the change and the progress. To put it simply, a before-and-after image should be available to be able to compare them and specify the progress toward the goal. Let us give an example. Company X has targeted at improving the overall productivity by 5 percent for the next year. After talking with them, we raise this question: "What/when/how will you measure the productivity to report the advancement to the goal?"

In line with the main point this chapter has formed around, ask questions, or to say it more suitably, dare to ask questions even from yourself. If there is no answer, then there are points needed to be clarified; there is miscomprehension required to be fixed; or there is a destination, but the path is needed to be drawn!

Case 15 – Company M, despite its efforts to resist against the incorporation of an agile approach, has been compelled to transform its approach in response to a customer's request.

- How can they formulate new strategies and goals?
- What should they pay attention to when forming the teams?
- What will be the consequences of this transformation?

The strategies regarding the scrum-based projects can be formulated with the help of the next model.

The Pentagon of Communication was developed for distributed team communication, particularly for projects with a scrum approach containing five dimensions of: competency, correlation, contentment, comprehension, and commitment (Amar et al., 2019).

NOTES

In a similar vein with the literature, the members on a team should be competent, especially their lead, their manager, or the scrum master. This is due to the nature of agile methods since the team members are empowered and the team is expected to be self-organized.

The other dimension is the relationship between the members. Agile teams are not like the order-do-hard structure teams when every member is afraid of discussing his/her ideas. Oppositely, the atmosphere is cozy but at the same time professional to encourage the team to share their ideas. Even during the daily meetings where the three questions are answered, the honest comments and explanations of the members are expected.

Commitment is the dimension that is usually overlooked in practice. It is for the reason that it is not understood well. Sometimes, during the training sessions, when we mention that we can begin the tasks right after the team commitment, we have many questions raised of which its main one is: "What does commitment mean in this context?"

*Commitment was suggested to include these components: planning, being prompt, and being flexible or accessible (*Amar et al., 2019*). To put it in simple words, being committed is the commitment to working under the agreed conditions.*

NOTES

Agile team members are expected to possess specific characteristics and skills like being a good team player and being good at communication and collaboration. This is valid for the agile team coach as well. He/she should bear particular skills. The problem we spotted is that companies turn to agile by altering the title of "project manager" with "agile coach" or "scrum master," and that's all!

Based on our observations and we are sure that you have encountered the same cases, not all great project managers are great agile coaches, and not all great agile coaches are great project managers! One serves the teams while the other orders and controls the team, and it is effort-taking to balance these approaches, nonetheless, not impossible!

In the following box, the skills of an IT project manager are brought.

Skill Categories of IT Project Managers were described as: client management, general management, communication, leadership, personal integrity, planning and control, team and systems development, and problem-solving (Napier et al., 2009).

NOTES

A well-known debate in strategic management is about strategy and structure; does strategy form the structure or the other way around?

Whatever is the case and what is your standpoint within this argument, the crystal clear issue here is that there should be alignment and harmony between the structure and strategy.

Taking a look at the practice, since the strategy is the side that is vital and life-saving to the organization, we usually suggest the companies to adjust their structure according to their strategies.

Coming to Case 15, unfortunately, the number of companies that have undergone agile transformation without any structural change is not low! The strict hierarchical structure is present with the old order-and-command system, and then they encourage the agile coach to stand near the team, not above it!

What is recommended to Company M may include, but it is not limited to these steps:

- Training the members of agile methodology.
- Justifying the need for changes, which is the hardest part since it is directly related to the inertia and the resistance to change that will consequently emerge.
- Smoothly turn into a more appropriate organizational structure that supports their strategies.
- Look closely for the effects of the changes and compare them with the predicted effects.
- Tracking the transformation process regularly.

NOTES

Changing the organizational structure is not a one-day task and trying to push the employees to implement and adapt to it is not recommended for the reason that it worsens the situation. The organizational structure should be depicted in alignment with the strategy and all the aspects should be reviewed and thought of. It can be initiated within the department and units based on the priority or in accordance with the willingness and readiness felt in the departments and units.

In companies, it is usually conducted by selecting a pilot department or a group of departments. This will help the companies to observe the changes, resistance, and outcome with a keen eye for any modification or alteration needed for further implementation.

The other advantage is that it soothes the resistance against the change; the employees against the changes will see the other departments, the change benefits, and the process implemented, and it may have positive effects on their perception of change. We have faced the cases within which the employees begin following the transformation very closely and are impatiently requesting and waiting for the transformation to embrace their departments and units as well.

NOTES

Never expect that something that has been done once and was expected to keep going that way is going the same way after some time!

Follow-up meetings, controls, and checks are what we execute a lot in the companies. Going back to the previous norms and the old ways of doing things is the reason for reassessments, reappraisals, and recertification apart, from keeping the company and individuals updated.

Even when providing consultancy services to a software company, months after the completion of the project, nothing would remain same, and you see that best practices, which you have spent so much time to justify their usage, convince the others to collaborate, and build all the infrastructure needed, have just been replaced partially or fully due to numerous reasons of those common ones are:

- *They were not practical.*
- *They were time-taking.*
- *We can go back to them when the recertification time comes.*
- *We have our own priorities.*
- *We don't have enough time and resources. It was just for the project period.*

Case 16 – Company N has delivered the software to its customers. There were issues that required more consideration, though, due to the time pressure and the project schedule, Company N decided on its delivery. Several months have passed since the delivery, and the maintenance costs are becoming higher and higher than expected.

How will you express this situation?

Technical debt is a term used to refer to many software quality problems related to accumulated software costs, and the results of a study showed that technical debt is mostly related to architectural choices at the very beginning of the Software Development Lifecycle (SDLC) (Ernst et al., 2015).

Nontechnical debt covers the dimensions of social, process, and people (Ahmad & Gustavsson, 2022).

NOTES

Given the information provided in the previous box, the problem is due to technical debt. When making decisions for such cases, it is better to contemplate these issues carefully:

- *How well can a short-term solution work?*
- *How long the solution can last?*
- *How much will be the cost to fix the raising problems due to the debt?*
- *Will the maintenance cost more?*
- *How can the debt and the maintenance cost become balanced?*
- *To what extent can we tolerate the technical debt?*

1.3 Defining the Target Situation

Consistent with the topic of this book, the targets we intend to set within strategic software quality management should bear two main characteristics:

- Goals and targets should be aligned with the strategies.
- Goals and targets should be compliant with the software quality management concepts.

Quality was mentioned as a concept covering many characteristics, and for this reason, it is illustrated within different models, capturing its numerous characteristics and the relationships that exist between them (Kassie & Singh, 2020).

NOTES

When you ask about the definition of quality, you will face many different views from a lot of diverse perspectives. There was a time, and for some, even now, that people reply to you that it is a subjective concept.

During years, researchers have attempted to find a precise definition for it and make it a standardized concept. The models of software quality can be outcomes of the efforts.

After the popularization of the agile method, some were baffled since quality was defined as customer-oriented. If the product meets the expectations of the customer and makes him/her satisfied, then we can conclude that the software is of good quality.

The clarification here should be that some requirements related to software are functional while the rest are nonfunctional.

The functional requirements are those related to the system and its components, whereas the nonfunctional requirements are quality attributes.

Given the quality models in Table 1.3, the quality attributes concentrate on how the system should realize the functional requirements.

Table 1.3 Software Quality Models

Number	*Software Quality Models*	*1st level*	*Notes*	*Reference*
1	McCall	Product revisions, transition, and operation.		McCall et al. (1977)
2	Boehm	As-is-utility, portability, and maintainability.		Boehm et al. (1976)
3	FURPS	Functionality, usability, reliability, performance, and supportability.		Al-Qutaish (2010) and Grady (1992)
4	Dromey	Correctness, internal, contextual, and descriptive properties.	These are properties of the product that affect quality.	Dromey (1996)
5	ISO 9126	Functionality, reliability, usability, efficiency, maintainability, and portability.	It was replaced by ISO/IEC 25010	Kassie & Singh (2020)
6	Kazman	Efficiency and modifiability.		(Suman & Wadhwa, 2014)

Software Product Quality can be interpreted variously when viewed by different roles involved in the software development process.

Software quality factors from a user's perspective were identified as: being function, being reliable, being usable and efficient, being maintainable and portable, being understandable, interoperability and operability, and bearing aesthetic characteristics (Singh & Kassie, 2018).

Quality attributes of the quality models were compared in different papers available in the literature (Singh, 2013; Suman & Wadhwa, 2014).

From a strategic point of view, *structure follows the strategy*, it is more consistent to align our processes with our strategies and goals. Therefore, within the scope of this chapter, first the targets should be set.

NOTES

Some of us have gotten used to using almost synonym words interchangeably, and this results in overlooking their subtle difference and their appropriate usage in more scientific and professional texts.

FROM VISION TO IMPLEMENTATION

Two opposite directions were drawn to show the flow: one for the thought and one for the work, where the direction of the thought was illuminated as: vision, goal, strategy, concept, planning, and execution, and the direction for the work is the other way around (Kolbusa, 2013).

In practice, targets are the output of the breakdown of goals. Goals are long-term and targets are planned for short-term achievements, usually accompanied with indicators to facilitate their measurement.

At the first step, the target situation should be defined taking both strategies and quality into account. Strategies are identified by the strategists; thus, we can just take the related objective key results (OKRs) from them. However, the quality attributes are needed to be specified whether they are selected based on a model or they are the combination of a model and customers' expectations. The quality team in collaboration with the analysis team can decide on the attributes and finalize the list.

At the second step, our existing processes list should be prepared. If the company has been established recently and no processes have been determined yet, processes can be defined based on the models available.

At the third step, Key Performance Indicators (KPIs) are determined for each process. There are myriads of indicators available for each phase of software development, and the right ones can be chosen among them.

KPI guides on actions required to achieve significant performance and a 12-step model was recommended for utilizing it (Parmenter, 2010).

At the fourth step, the contribution of the processes to the relevant OKR and the quality attributes are specified.

OKR Framework is a methodology of management by objectives (MBO); objectives portray the company strategies at a high level; key results specify measurable outcomes that can be verified against the previously outlined objectives (Criado et al., 2024).

The steps mentioned can be performed utilizing the framework in Table 1.4.

Table 1.4 Target Situation Definition Framework

					Current Contribution to						*Targeted Contribution to*						*Action Plan(s) with QA and OKR Codes*
					Quality Attributes (QA)			*OKR*			*QA*			*OKR*			
Phase	*Process*	*Input*	*Output*	*KPI*	*QA 1*	*QA 2*	*QA 3*	*OKR 1*	*OKR 2*	*OKR 3*	*QA 1*	*QA 2*	*QA 3*	*OKR 1*	*OKR 2*	*OKR 3*	
					X				x		x	x			x	x	
						x	x			x	x	x	X				

At the fifth step, the action plans are agreed upon and added to the table together with their corresponding quality attributes and OKRs.

NOTES

It is worth introducing the concept, which is usually confused with KPI.

Key Result Indicator (KRI) *provides information on what an employee has performed regarding a critical success factor, which entails customer profitability and satisfaction, employee satisfaction, pre-tax net profit, and return on capital employed (ROCE)* (Parmenter, 2010).

KRI is mainly used by the top management, execution board, and the board of directors.

Sometimes, new processes should be designed or existing processes should be updated. The next information box can be of help through this action.

Process Design can be performed by considering trigger, action, and value proposition (Grisold et al., 2022).

The change in the processes can be determined and documented using Table 1.5. The approvers are dependent on the structure of the organization. The important issues here are:

- Justification of the need for a new process or the need for modification.
- Evaluation of the request objectively by different peers.
- Determination of the processes affected by the change and the extent of the effects.
- Communication of change to the related employees and stakeholders.
- Perform follow-up controls to see whether the process has met its desired purpose or not.

Urgency and importance levels can be determined as high, medium, and low, and the column related to Ds can be filled out according to the four D boxs, a version of the Eisenhower matrix (Ngandam Mfondoum et al., 2019).

As it is seen in the table, the last four columns are about the people playing different roles concerning the decisions made. The columns colored in darker gray, the right six columns, are required to be filled out by the evaluators.

Table 1.5 Request for Process Creation or Modification

Request Type		*Justification*													
Creation	*Modification*	*Improvement*	*Innovation*	*Any Reference or Best Practice*	*Urgency Level*	*Importance Level*	*Processes Affected*	*Impact on each Process*	*4Ds: Do, Decide, Delegate, Delete*	*Actions Plans*	*Responsible*	*Accountable*	*Consulted*	*Informed*

There can be diverse approaches here: first, the form can be given to various evaluators by the quality expert and then collected to see their decisions and go on with the majority. This can be like a peer review process.

The other approach is to conduct meetings on a regular basis if: the number of change requests are high or on the need basis in case the numbers are low, and then ask the participants to discuss the matter, and reach, and record the decision in the table.

NOTES

Some companies have already defined the Change Committee or Change Board internally. It is apart from the Change Control Board (CCB), which tracks the changes in the project in terms of scope, budget, and schedule, but actually inspired by it.

Quality, process, excellence, or any related department can take the responsibility of forming such a committee consisting of numerous and diverse experts and professionals on each phase of the software development, making it is a cross-functional committee. This cross-functionality nature assists the committee to make the righteous and context-appropriate decision regarding the requests made.

Designing new processes can be done by using another tool called SIPOC. SIPOC can be prepared for each of the SDLC phases.

SIPOC Diagram is a tool within the Six Sigma approach where different aspects of a process, including supplier, input, process, output, and customer, can be well pictured (Redzic & Baik, 2006).

It is a simple but, at the same time, a comprehensive tool that clarifies a process in detail.

Likewise, it can also be adopted for the identification of the problems within the existing processes; to determine whether the input, output, and providers of input and recipients of outputs can be recognized or not. The difficulties or inabilities with the determination of these aspects can be implied as the existence of a problem associated with one or several of these issues:

- The process has not been defined precisely.
- The process lacks some aspects; for instance, it has not been determined where the inputs come from or who is in charge of the inputs.
- The process has not been updated, thus, it is different from what is executed practically. As a result, the aspects cannot be pinpointed.

NOTES

Almost all software companies have predefined processes. Some record it, and some just own it as part of their organizational knowledge.

The first critical point is to have written processes. What we mean is not to write it on paper. There are many tools accessible for portraying and keeping records of the processes within a company. This brings many advantages to the company of which the most important on is to detect the issues with the processes easily.

The second critical point is to keep them updated. The number of companies that have once created the documentation related to their processes and left it on the shelves of the library (not literally) is unfortunately high. Again, as part of the responsibility of the quality, process, excellence, or any relevant department, the documentation of the processes should be checked regularly to see if there is a need for any updates on the documentation, or perhaps, there might be a need for a new tool!

1.4 Gap Analysis

Gap analysis is one of the most argumentative, and at the same time, widespread concepts in software companies. It is performed in attempt to understand the difference between the target and the current situation as implied by its name.

NOTES

Problems that we usually spot in software companies in terms of the conduction of gap analysis are:

- *Some companies do not have a written or predefined process to conduct gap analysis, and it is being done in different formats, sometimes unfitted with the context. As a result, the output of the analysis would not be applicable in reality.*
- *There are models and frameworks for performing gap analysis, and some companies do not approach any of these.*
- *Sufficient time is not allocated to the gap analysis, and it leads to incomplete and superficial findings.*
- *Tools have been developed for doing the gap analysis and they simplify the process for the company, although not many companies are leveraging them.*
- *Based on experience, we know that the process, which has been not defined well or has been mentioned as optional, hardly takes place in a company. Therefore, gap analysis should be both stated and kept as a mandatory step within companies.*
- *The other common problem is the lack of support from the top management. We have received feedback from the employees, which points to the lack of attention and support from top management. Some of these feedbacks are:*
  - *Why am I preparing a report if no one is going to read it?*
  - *Why should I do gap analysis when it is not even really asked for?*
  - *The other case is about having inexperienced employees running the analysis, and if it is not researched well and enough time is not spent on the learning process, again, the obtained results will not be reliable.*

Gap Analysis Data Collection was noted to have two pillars: interviews and analysis of documentation (Amaral & Faria, 2010).

A model for gap analysis consists of four steps: preparation, information collection, information confirmation, and creation and presentation of the report; data collection of their study was done through interviews, conversations, and artifacts (Amaral & Faria, 2010).

Myriads of templates can be found on the internet for gap analysis. Approaching gap analysis from both strategic management and quality management viewpoints can bring about some differences to the template

Table 1.6 Gap Analysis from Strategic Quality Management Perspective

Process Name	*Current KPI*	*Target KPI*	*Description (If KPI Is Not Available)*	*Gap (Percentage)*	*Priority For Process*			*Improvement Action Plan*	*Scope of the Effect*		*Final Decision*	*Responsible*	*Accountable*	*Consulted*	*Informed*
					L	*M*	*H*		*QA No.*	*OKR No.*					

since it should entail both strategy and quality-related aspects. A sample template is shared in Table 1.6.

The description column is filled out if KPIs were not determined for the process previously. This points at the need to identify the right KPIs for the process or whether, in rare cases, KPI might not be applicable to the process only after careful examination.

The priority can be marked as high, medium, or low.

Improvement action plan should include the details of actions devised for filling the gap, written neatly and precisely.

The possible effects of the improvements on quality attributes (QA) and OKRs should be noted by writing the corresponding number of QA and OKRs.

Final decision regarding the improvement action plan can take these three forms: accepted, rejected, and further research required. The four last columns are completed with regard to the decision:

- If the decision is "rejected," consulted and informed columns will be populated.
- If the decision is "accepted," all four columns have to be completed.
- If the decision is "further research required," the last four columns will be filled out regarding the research, or to clarify it within an example, the person who is responsible for the research will be mentioned or the one who is accountable for running the research will be added.

NOTES

We believe that a process, as it has fixed parts like input and output, should be quantifiable. Measurement is of great significance in drawing the path, creating the strategies, and improving our initiatives. Without constant measurement, we would not know where we were, where we are, and where we will be. Even predictions of the future are also done by looking at the values of the past and present like trying to find a trend or pattern within the data. Hence, as consultants, we always suggest the companies incorporate indicators, metrics, and measures while elucidating their processes.

We confront cases where there is resistance against the determination of KPIs for a process or it seems too hard to define KPIs. The reasons are mainly due to the ambiguity with the process, the triviality of the process, the fear of information overload, or the insufficient knowledge and skill of the employees about the process and KPI. To overcome these issues, our recommendations can be outlined this way:

- *Write the processes as clearly as possible.*
- *Be consistent in the process definition approach. For instance, if you use SIPOC, use it for all processes, not some.*
- *Attempt to determine measures and KPIs for processes. Even in the worst situation, the percentage of completion can be a KPI!*
- *Do not skip the processes and their aspects if you were not successful at the first try. Consult with other professionals and experts, widen the scope of your research, and get inspiration from best practices.*
- *If you were told that a process is trivial, then you can pinpoint the critical processes by using methods like MCDM and restrict the use of KPIs to these critical processes. This is usually preferred by companies with a wide range of processes, and it is kind of a matter of scaling.*
- *Do not forget that if you do not know a process from your heart, it will be an arduous task to define measures for it.*
- *Unfortunately, this is the situation in many companies where quality experts are compelled to prepare the list of KPI processes. Contrary to this misbelief, the quality expert is only accountable for this task, not responsible! The process owners who are technical people and have deep knowledge of the process hold the main responsibility for preparing the KPI list related to their processes and forwarding them to the quality experts, process excellence experts, or any related positions, who will then compile all the received lists and add them to the documentation as part of his/her responsibility.*

References

Ahmad, M. O., & Gustavsson, T. (2022). The Pandora's Box of Social, Process, and People Debts in Software Engineering. *Journal of Software: Evolution and Process*, 36, 1–24.

Al-Qutaish, R. E. (2010). Quality Models in Software Engineering Literature: An Analytical and Comparative Study. *Journal of American Science*, 6(3), 166–175.

Amar, H., Rafi-ul-Shan, P. M., & Adegbile, A. (2019). Towards A 5c Theory of Communication for Scrum-Based Distributed Projects. *BAM2019 Conference Proceedings*. Birmingham: The British Academy of Management (BAM).

Amaral, L. M., & Faria, J. P. (2010). A Gap Analysis Methodology for the Team Software. 2010 Seventh International Conference on the Quality of Information and Communications Technology (pp. 424–429). Porto, Portugal: IEEE Computer Society.

Archer, N., & Ghasemzadeh, F. (1999). An Integrated Framework for project Portfolio Selection. *International Journal of Project Management*, 17(4), 207–216.

Bahli, B., & Rivard, S. (2003). The Information Technology Outsourcing Risk: A Transaction Cost and Agency Theory-Based Perspective. *Journal of Information Technology, 18(3),* 211–221.

Barney, J. (1991). Firm Reources and Sustained Competetive Advantage. *Journal of Management*, 17(1), 99–120.

Barney, J. B., & Hesterly, W. S. (2008). *Strategic Management and Competitive Advantage: Concepts and Cases*. New Jersey: Pearson Prentice Hall.

Beecham, S., Hall, T., & Rainer, A. (2003). Software Process Improvement Problems in Twelve Software Companies: An Empirical Analysis. *Empirical Software Engineering*, 8, 7–42.

Bergena, M., & Peteraf, M. A. (2002). Competitor Identification and Competitor Analysis: A Broad-Based Managerial Approach. *Managerial and Decision Economics*, 23(4–5), 157–159.

Boehm, B. W., Brown, J. R., & Lipow, M. (1976). Quantitative Evaluation of Software Quality. *Proceedings of the 2nd International Conference on Software Engineering* (pp. 592–605). San Francisco, California: IEEE Computer Society Press.

Boja, C. (2011). IT Clusters as a Special Type of Industrial Clusters. 184 Informatica Economica, 15(2), 184–193.

Cardeal, N., & António, N. (2012). Valuable, Rare, Inimitable Resources and Rrganization (VRIO) Resources or Valuable, Rare, Inimitable Resources(VRI) Capabilities: What Leads to Competitive Advantage?. *African Journal of Business Management*, 10159–10170.

Chen, M.-J. (1996). Competitor Analysis and Interfirm Rivalry: Toward a Theoretical Integration. *The Academy of Management Review*, 21(1), 100–134.

Chiaburu, D. S., & Tekleab, A. G. (2005). Individual and Contextual Influences on Multiple Dimensions of Training Effectiveness. *Journal of European Industrial Training*, 29(8), 604–626.

Colquitt, J. A., Conlon, D. E., Wesson, M. J., Porter, C. O., & Ng, K. Y. (2001). Justice at the Millennium: A Meta-Analytic Review of 25 Years of Organizational Justice Research. *Journal of Applied Psychology*, 86(3), 425–445.

Criado, J. M., Gutierrez Peña, G., Garzás, J., Cano, E. L., Lena, M., & Moguerza, J. (2024). Exploring the Effectiveness of OKRs in Enhancing Company Objectives: A Comparative Study. *Exploring the Effectiveness of OKRIEEE Engineering Management Review*, 1–8.

Dromey, R. G. (1996). Concerning the Chimera (Software Quality). *IEEE Software*, 13(1), 33–43.

Ellram, L. M. (1995). Total Cost of Ownership:. *International Journal of Physical Distribution & Logistics*, 25(8), 4–23.

ENRÍQUEZ-DE-LA-O, J. F. (2015). Resource-based View and Dynamic Capabilities: Achieving Competitive Advantage through Internal Resources and Competences. *Vezetéstudomány/Budapest Management Review*, 46(11), 50–61.

Ernst, N. A., Bellomo, S., Ozkaya, I., Nord, R. L., & Gorton, I. (2015). Measure It? Manage It? Ignore It? Software Practitioners and Technical Debt. *Proceedings of the 10th Joint Meeting on Foundations of Software Engineering.* (pp. 50–60). Bergamo: Proceedings of the 10th Joint Meeting on Foundations of Software Engineering.

Fernandez-Escobedo, R., Eguía-Peña, B., & Aldaz-Odriozola, L. (2024). Economic Agglomeration in the Age of Industry 4.0: Developing a Digital Industrial Cluster as a New Policy Tool for the Digital World. *Competitiveness Review: An International Business Journal*, 34(3), 538–558.

Fidanboy, M. (2022). *Organizations and Complex Adaptive Systems.* New York: Routledge.

Garud, R., Kumaraswamy, A., & Karnøe, P. (2010). Path Dependence or Path Creation? *Journal of Management Studies*, 47(4), 760–774.

Gáspár, T. (2011). Path Dependency and Path Creation in a Strategic Perspective. *Journal of Futures Studies*, 15(4), 93–108.

Grady, R. B. (1992). *Practical Software Metrics for Project Management and Process Improvement.* New Jersey: Prentice Hall.

Grisold, T., Groß, S., Stelzl, K., Vom Brocke, J., Mendling, J., Ro¨glinger, M., & Rosemann, M. (2022). The Five Diamond Method for Explorative Business Process. *Business & Information Systems Engineering*, 64(2), 149–166.

Grosskopf, S. (1993). Efficiency and Productivity. In H. O. Fried, C. A. Lovell, & S. S. Schmidt, *The Measurement of Productive Efficiency: Techniques and Applications* (pp. 160–194). New York: Oxford University Press.

Guzeller, C. O., & Celiker, N. (2019). Examining the Relationship between Organizational Commitment and Turnover Intention via a Meta-analysis. *International Journal of Culture, Tourism and Hospitality Research*, 14(1), 102–120.

Hammer, M. (1990). Reengineering Work: Don't Automate, Obliterate. *Harvard Business Review* , 68(4), 104–112.

Hannan, M. T., & Freeman, J. (1989). *Organizational Ecology.* Cambridge, MA: Harvard University Press.

Huijgens, H., Van Solingen, R., & Van Deursen, A. (2014). How to Build a Good Practice Software Project Portfolio? *36th International Conference on Software Engineering, ICSE Companion 2014 – Proceedings: Software Engineering in Practice Track (SEIP)* (pp. 64–73). Hyderabad, India: IEEE.

Jain, A. (2015). SWOT Analysis in Thirukkural: Comparative Analysis with Humphrey SWOT Matrix. *Journal of Business and Management (IOSR-JBM)*, 7(1), 31–34.

Jensen, M. C., & Meckling, W. H. (1976). Theory of the Firm: Managerial Behavior, Agency Costs and Ownership Structure. *Journal of Financial Economics*, 3(4), 305–360.

Kaiser, R., Futami, A. H., Valentina, L. V., & Oliveira, M. A. (2019). Development of a Managerial Tool for Prioritization and Selection of Portfolio Projects Using the Analytic Hierarchy Process Methodology in Software Companies. *Gestão & Produção*, 26, 1–13.

Kano, N., Seraku, N., Takahashi, F., & Tsuji, S. (1984). Attractive Quality and Must-be Quality. *Journal of the Japanese Society for Quality Control*, 39–48.

Kaplan, R. S., & Norton, D. (1992). The Balanced Scorecard: Measures that Drive Performance. *Harvard Business Review*, 70, 71–79.

Kassie, N. B., & Singh, J. (2020). A Study on Software Quality Factors and Metrics to Enhance Software Quality Assurance. *International Journal of Productivity and Quality Management*, 29(1), 24–44.

Kolbusa, M. (2013). *Implementation Management: High Speed Strategy Implementation*. Heidelberg: Springer Berlin, Heidelberg.

Kontio, J., Lehtola, L., & Bragge, J. (2004). Using the Focus Group Method in Software Engineering: Obtaining Practitioner and User Experiences. *Proceedings of the 2004 International Symposium on Empirical Software Engineering (ISESE'04)* (pp. 271–280). Redondo Beach, CA: IEEE.

Lee, R., & Dale, B. G. (1998). Business Process Management: A Review and Evaluation. *Business Process Management*, 4(3), 214–225.

Mack, N., Woodsong, C., MacQueen, K. M., Guest, G., & Namey, E. (2005). *Qualitative Research Methods: A Data Collector's Field Guide*. North Carolina: Family Health International.

Madhani, P. M. (2009). Resource Based View (RBV) of Competitive Advantage An Overview. In P. M. Madhani, *Resource Based View: Concepts and Practices* (pp. 3–22). Hyderabad, India: Icfai University Press.

McCall, J. A., Richards, P. K., & Walters, G. F. (1977). *Factors in Software Quality: Concept and Definitions of Software Quality*. New York: ROME Air Development Center, Air Force Systems Command, Griffiss Air Force Base.

Meyer, J. P., & Allen, N. J. (1991). A Three-Component Conceptualizaiton of Organizational Commitment. *Human Resource Management Review*, 1(1), 61–89.

Mikulic´, J., & Prebezˇac, D. (2011). A Critical Review of Techniques for Classifying Quality Attributes in the Kano model. *Managing Service Quality*, 21(1), 46–66.

Napier, N. P., Keil, M., & Tan, F. B. (2009). IT Project Managers' Construction of Successful Project Management Practice: A Repertory Grid Investigation. *Information Systems Journal*, 19(3), 255–282.

Ngandam Mfondoum, A. H., Tchindjang, M., Mefire Mfondoum, J. V., & Makouet, I. (2019). Eisenhower Matrix * Saaty AHP = Strong Actions Prioritization? Theoretical Literature and Lessons Drawn from Empirical Evidences. *IATSD Journal for Advanced Research in Applied Sciences*, 13–27.

O'Neill, P., & Sohal, A. S. (1999). Business Process Reengineering: A Review of Recent Literature. *Technovation*, 19(9), 571–581.

Parmenter, D. (2010). *Key Performance Indicators: Developing, Implementing, and Using Winning KPIs*. New Jersey: Wiley, John Wiley & Sons, Inc.

Pati, N., & Desai, M. S. (2005). Conceptualizing Strategic Issues in Information Technology Outsourcing. *Information Management & Computer Security*, 13(4), 281–296.

Pfeffer, J., & Salancik, G. R. (2003). *The External Control of Organizations: A Resource Dependence Perspective*. New York: Stanford University Press.

Porter, M. E. (1998). Clusters and the New Economics of Competition. *Harvard Business Review*, 1–32.

Puyt, R. W., Lie, F. B., & Wilderom, C. P. (2023). The Origins of SWOT Analysis. *Long Range Planning*, 56(3), 1–24.

Redzic, C., & Baik, J. (2006). Six Sigma Approach in Software Quality Improvement. *Proceedings of the Fourth International Conference on Software Engineering Research Management and Applications (SERA'06)* (pp. 396–406). Saettle: Fourth International Conference on Software Engineering Research.

Shenhar, A. J., & Dov, D. (2007). *Reinventing Project Management; The Diamond Approach to Successful Growth and Innovation*. Boston, Massachusetts: Harvard Business School Press.

Silaban, N., & Syah, T. Y. (2018). The Influence of Compensation and Organizational Commitment. *Journal of Business and Management (IOSR-JBM)*, 1–6.

Singh, I. (2013). *International Journal on Recent and Innovation Trends in Computing and Communication*. Different Software Quality Model, 1(5), 438–442.

Singh, J., & Kassie, N. B. (2018). User's Perspective of Software Quality. *Proceedings of the 2nd International conference on Electronics, Communication and Aerospace Technology (ICECA 2018)* (pp. 1958–1963). Coimbatore, India: IEEE.

SumanWadhwa, M. (2014). A Comparative Study of Software Quality Models. *International Journal of Computer Science and Information Technologies (IJCSIT), 5(4)*, 5634–5638.

Tuckman, B. W. (1965). Developmental Sequence in Small Groups. *Psychological Bulletin*, 63(6), 384–399.

Ulrich, D., & Lake, D. (1991). Organizational Capability: Creating Competetive Advantage. *Academy of Management Executive*, 5(1), 77–92.

Van der Klink, M. R., & Streumer, J. N. (2002). Effectivesnesss of On-the-Job Training. *Journal of European Industrial Training*, 26(2-3-4), 196–199.

Williamson, O. E. (2014). The Transaction Cost Economics Project. *Montenegrin Journal of Economics*, 10(1), 7–11.

Wilson, E. J. (1994). The Relative Importance of Supplier Selection Criteria: A Review and Update. *International Journal of Purchasing and Materials Management*, 30(2), 35–41.

Yalabik, Z. Y., Rossenberg, Y. v., Kinnie, N., & Swart, J. S. (2015). Engaged and Committed? The Relationship between Work Engagement and Commitment in Professional Service Firms. *The International Journal of Human Resource*, 26(12), 1602–1621.

Yildiz, R. O., & Esmer, S. (2023). Talent Management Strategies and Functions: A Systematic Review. *Industrial and Commercial Training*, 55(1), 93–11.

Yüksel, İ. (2012). Developing a Multi-Criteria Decision Making Model for PESTEL. *International Journal of Business and Management, 7(24)*, 52–66.

Zairi, M. (1997). Business Process Management: A Boundaryless Approach to Modern Competitiveness. *Business Process Management*, 3(1), 64–80.

Chapter 2

Improvement Areas

2.1 Introduction

This chapter focuses on improvement areas, and different methods and tools are described to be benefited from, but before that, let us discuss what we mean by improvement areas.

Existing processes in a software company have to be checked for their efficiency from time to time. A process which was efficient once might not be of that usefulness later. It is valid for approaches, frameworks, and models as well. This is the reason behind the versioning and updating them by the authorized organizations from time to time. A vast number of academic studies have been investigating the modification or alteration of the existing models.

Coming back to the context of a company, what we suggest the companies do is to allocate sources to follow and gain fresh information on the recent updates to the models, standards, frameworks, and trends, and share it with the relevant employees inside a company by holding workshops, talks, or any other kinds of communication of the knowledge like posters or internal assessments. This unit can be the research and development unit, which we are already familiar with.

Unfortunately, the idea of creating such a unit is not welcomed by many software companies, and one of their justifications is that they do not produce physical products; hence, there will be no need for such a unit.

Their other explanation is that they are not a big software company like many famous ones that we all know, and allocating resources will be a burden for them in terms of budget.

We, as consultants, have a hard time convincing the companies of these kinds of changes. Senior management falsely believes that the employees

DOI: 10.4324/9781003491606-2

update their knowledge related to their working field and bring that knowledge into the company, reflecting it in the processes, nonetheless, this is not the case in most companies unless relevant objective key results (OKRs) are defined and related strategies are formulated and implemented. Even in this case, there is always a way to show the unreal image, as stepping outside the comfort zone is not the preference and tendency of a vast number of employees.

The other solution is to recruit individuals who are proactive and passionate about their working area; those who learn if they are not told to learn and take steps toward improvements even if they are not asked for. It is noteworthy that recruitment of proactive employees will not be a complete solution if the organizational culture does not value this behavior and no mechanisms exist within the organization to foster proactive learning. Thus, cultivating the learning culture in the organization is of paramount importance.

To sum up, there rest some options in front of the software companies if they want to improve their processes:

- Allocate resources with expertise in process improvement.
- Provide training and perform effective assessments to keep their employees updated on their specific topics.
- Foster the introduction of new solutions and ideas by motivating the employees and offering incentives.

And it should not be ignored that intrinsic motivation is the real fuel for individuals to research, learn, and share knowledge.

2.2 Collection of Data

When collecting data is viewed from a scientific perspective, it will be in the forms of qualitative and quantitative data collection. Narrowing down the topic to software development makes us think of software metrics at the first place.

NOTES

If you ask consultants of software companies about the types of data, they might come up with answers like software metrics, quality assurance (QA) metrics, coverage, and so on, all of which are almost among quantitative data.

On the other hand, if you ask them which type of data they prefer to have for making decisions, they again will most probably reply "quantitative data!"

This made us think that the reason is the respondent! They are technical people, mostly engineers, who have worked with numbers and feel at ease with working with them.

The other probable explanation is that quantitative data is perceived as more objective when compared with qualitative data.

Our suggestion here is not advising any type of data, since the user knows which type is suitable for the intended use, however, what we want to emphasizes is to check the quality of data either qualitative or quantitative.

Data Quality consists of dimensions including being relevant with the goals and the needs, timeliness, being consistent, complete, and accurate (Pansara, 2023).

The importance of high-quality data should not be underestimated as the high-level decisions of companies are made based on the data collected from the operational levels of a company. These data guide the strategists in the choice of future strategies. The next information box briefly mentions some of the possible problems resulting from the data of poor quality.

Poor Data Quality may lead to issues with finance, the public image of the company, the efficiency of the operations, laws and regulations, and opportunities (Pansara, 2023).

We found our classification of the data sources based on basic parts of an organization.

Five Basic Parts of an Organization were portrayed as: technical staff, technical and administrative support staff, middle management, and top management (Mintzberg, 1980; Daft, 2008).

Let us elucidate the topic with some examples.

Data from the technical staff may include software metrics and key performance indicators (KPI) of the processes.

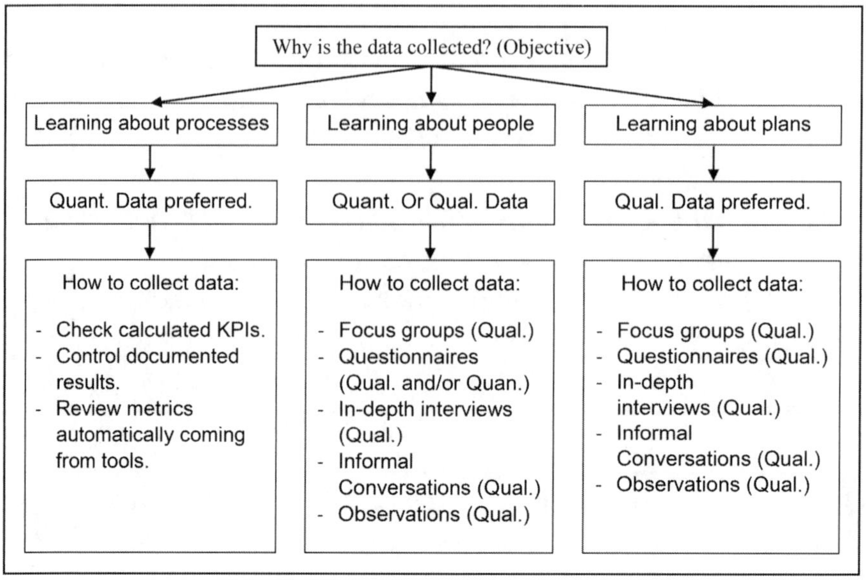

Figure 2.1 Data collection method selection. *Abbreviations:* Quant., Quantitative; Qual., Qualitative.

Technical support staff provides data on areas such as the environment, new regulations and laws, competitors, new innovations, models, and/or frameworks.

Administrative support staff owns data related to employees, workplace, finance and financial issues, trainings, and assets of the organization.

Middle management collects the data from other units and creates unified data at a higher level to be presented to the top management for decision-making.

Top management data entail goals, objectives, strategies, plans, and future initiatives, some of which are classified.

Figure 2.1 will be of help with deciding which data collection method is appropriate in your context.

2.3 Analysis of Data

Analysis of the **quantitative data** in a software company can be done for two different purposes.

First can be to show a trend in the data, for example, the number of information security risks detected after risk assessment has dropped from 90 to 70, and from 70 to 55 during the last three years. It implies a downward trend and can be interpreted as that the initiatives have taken place have been effective, and it is predicted to result in a decrease in the number of risks in the next few years. This prediction is based on the primary interpretation. The case must be analyzed closely and carefully next to investigate the influencing factors. For instance, initiatives were taken during these three years targeting enhancing the information security practices of the company, which will be completed at the end of this year, and no more new initiatives have already been planned for the next year apart from performing the existing practices.

The **rule** here can be to check the quantitative data, examine the context the data extracted from, and review all the contextual factors influencing the data for any probable changes over time.

Second purpose can be to demonstrate the difference between the values set as the target and the values obtained in actual. Visualizing this difference or showing it in numbers can provide managers with beneficial data for decision-making. What should not be ignored again is that the context should be reviewed again and the probable affecting factors should be listed, with their effects outlined. An example of quantitative data analysis is brought in Figure 2.2.

The details related to which tools to choose for the visualization of what kind of data exceeds the boundaries of the scope of this book.

Analysis of the **qualitative data** can be much more time-consuming. The steps of the analysis briefly are:

- preparing the data;
- using predefined themes or defining themes based on the data;
- categorizing the data under these themes;

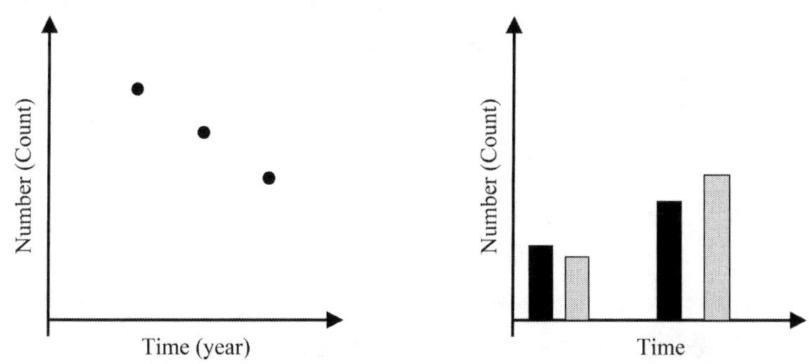

Figure 2.2 Example of quantitative data analysis.

- seeking for patterns, differences, similarities, and relationships within the themes; and
- visualizing and reporting the data.

Results from qualitative data analysis can be like this: 20 percent of the participants were satisfied with the talent management program; or "insufficient" and synonym words were the adjectives used to describe the talent management program characteristic by 30 percent of the respondents.

2.4 Identification of Improvement Areas

The third section of this chapter concentrates on the ways and methods to identify the improvement areas within a software company. To say it in simple words, first, a cause of a problem should be detected, and then the improvement initiatives and actions will be planned and started. Thus, with this taken for granted, we review some popular and common tools, methods, and techniques to find the causes of problems in software companies.

Cause Effect Analysis (CE) begins with listing all possible causes, and subsequently, the highly probable ones are extracted through brainstorming (Sanches et al., 2015).

Brainstorming is a method when several people are gathered together with the aim of producing ideas by concentrating on a specific subject; the presence of a moderator and the questions that work as triggers (Singer et al., 2008) help with realizing the process of deep thinking and seeking more specific answers.

NOTES

Brainstorming method is usually preferred by small companies or small departments or when the number of causes is low. Utilization of this method in other cases can result in almost unending lists and lengthy brainstorming sessions, which is the loss of time and effort.

This method can also be chosen for situations where pinpointing the causes and their probabilities do not seem easy, and there is a need for a brainstorming session to extract the underlying causes.

Table 2.1 Cause and Effect Matrix Template

		Importance to Customers (Weights)	*Weight 1*	*Weight 2*	
		Process Output	*Output 1*	*Output 2*	*Total*
SDLC Phase Name	Process Input		A	C	D
Phase 1	Input 1		B		
Phase 2	Input 2				

A more quantifiable method is to use a cause and effect matrix, which can be tailored based on the need and the context. A sample matrix is brought above.

Cause and Effect Matrix is a mathematical depiction of cause-and-effect relationships among variables; a management support tool, helping managers with conveying their grasp of complex issues clearly (Sanches et al., 2015). Cause and effect matrix template is shown in Table 2.1.

Weights related to the importance can be given based on the Likert scale. The correlation can be pointed out as 1 for low, 3 for medium, and 5 for high.

- Cell A represents the impact of input 1 on output 1, while cell B shows the impact of input 2 on output 1 if applicable.
- Cell C includes the impact of input 1 on output 2 if applicable.
- Cell D is filled out after completing the following calculation:

$$\text{Cell A value} \times \text{Weight 1} + \text{Cell C value} \times \text{Weight 2} = \text{Cell D value}$$

The last column shows the calculation results. This column can be used for prioritization of the causes, determining the improvement areas, and planning the corrective actions accordingly.

The next tool which is known to many is Pareto analysis.

Pareto Analysis is a quality control tool that illustrates the frequency of causes from the highest *f* to the lowest where the cumulative percentage of 80 is labeled as trivial or "useful many," and the other 20 percent is named as "vital few" (Karuppusami & Gandhinathan, 2006).

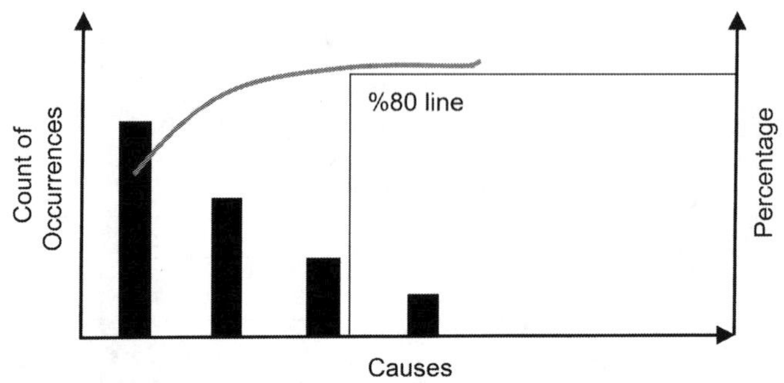

Figure 2.3 Simplified Pareto chart.

A simplified view of a Pareto analysis is brought next in Figure 2.3.

Almost always, we confront more than one problem, and consequently, there might exist more than one distinct cause. Having to deal with numerous causes necessitates a classification technique. A tree-based method is one of these.

Tree-Based Methods are employed for classifying. These methods were applied to the software context for grouping the failures with the same cause by using two techniques of dendrograms and classification trees in the form of a decision tree (Francis et al., 2004).

A general view of a tree-based method is represented in Figure 2.4. The benefits of such classification are the following:

- Clarity and ease of comprehension and interpretation.
- Representation of a basis for improvement area grouping.
- Ability to pinpoint the causes of causes.
- Narrowing down the locus of focus to groups with the most causes.
- Facilitation in the recognition of where the bottlenecks rest.

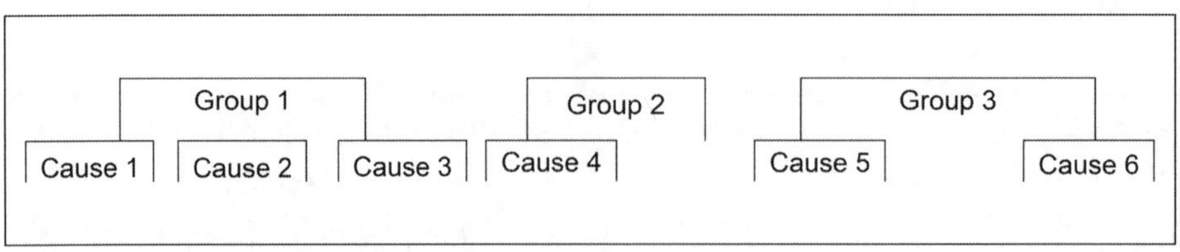

Figure 2.4 Tree-based method cause classification.

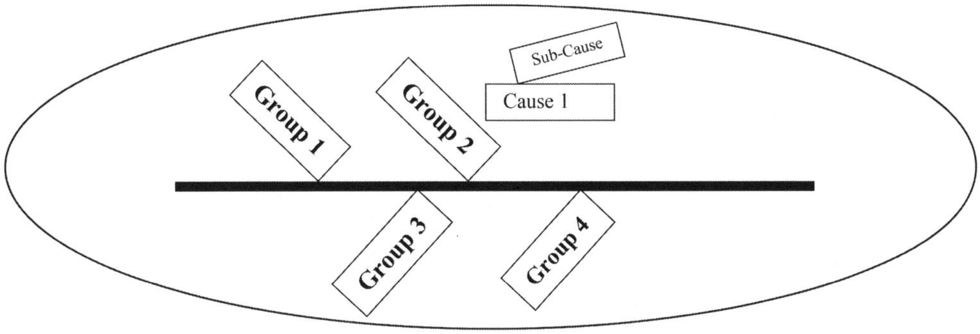

Figure 2.5 General view of a fishbone diagram.

The outcome of using this tool can be employed in planning for the actions concerning the improvement areas. It can be directly used to depict a picture of the causes of the problems and the categories in which most causes lie.

Another famous tool known by different names is the fishbone diagram.

Fishbone Diagram is a tool for root cause analysis (RCA) categorizing causes under four groups starting with M, which are man, machine, material, and environment, and one group beginning with E as the environment (Sakdiyah et al., 2022). A general view of it is depicted in Figure 2.5.

A term which software testers and developers are so familiar with is "root cause analysis."

Root Cause Analysis (RCA) is mainly adopted for detecting the origins of defects within the software development with the following advantages:

- avoiding the recurrence of the defects,
- advancement and enrichment of the processes,
- enhancement of organizational learning, and
- minimizing and mitigating risks (Pargaonkar, 2022).

Consistent with Ishikawa's suggestion on applying PDCA to initiatives concerning process improvement, RCA was implemented accordingly:

- Analyze problem.
- Execute countermeasures.
- Check for reduction in RCs and progress.
- Maintain improvements and incorporate them into the quality management system (Damele et al., 1996).

PCDA is a method comprising of the steps of plan, check, do, and act, which is a widely used tool for quality improvement that can be of help in different cycles such as the planning cycle and RCA cycle (Hasan & Hossain, 2018).

RCA can be adopted for detecting problems in plans, processes, and problems other than software and its defects.

5 Whys is another technique for cause identification which is commonly employed for continuous improvement.

5 Whys is another technique for RCA whose origin was stated to go back to Toyota Production System (TPS) (Card, 2016).

Repeating the "Why?" question five times can assist in discovering the root cause of a problem and facilitate addressing it effectively (Ohno, 1988).

A 5-why-based RCA table is brought next, which can be applied to different phases and contexts in software companies (Table 2.2).

The causes begin from general and then they become more detailed and deeper. Improvement areas and action plans are suggested to be performed starting from the last cause to solve the problem underlying all the layers and subsequently, come up and up in terms of the depth of the causes. This approach to resolving the problems will be much easier and more effective since the deepest cause is addressed sooner. Figure 2.6 depicts this approach.

Table 2.2 5-Why-Based RCA

Problem	*W1 Cause*	*W2 Cause*	*W3 Cause*	*W4 Cause*	*W5 Cause*	*Improvement Area(s)*	*Action Plan(s)*	*Responsible*	*Accountable*	*Consulted*	*Informed*
						W5	W5				
						W4	W4				
						W3	W3				
						W2	W2				
						W1	W1				

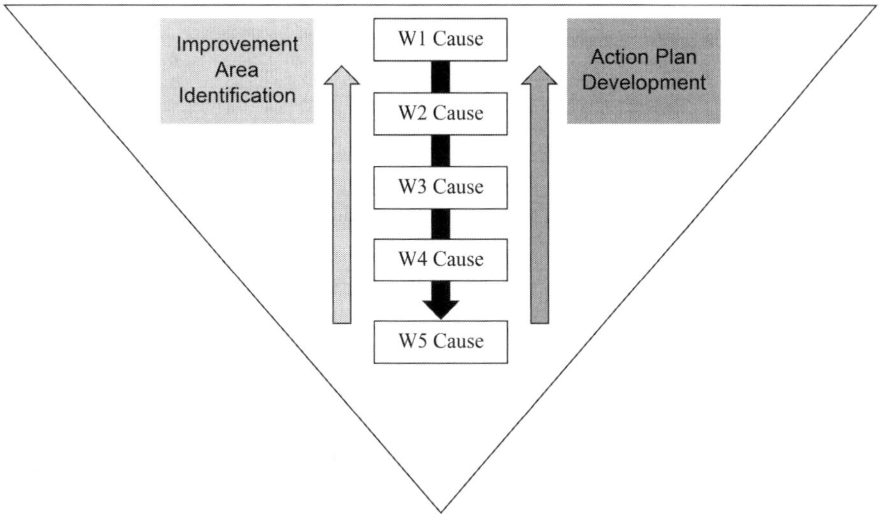

Figure 2.6 Approach toward cause, improvement area, and action plan.

The following two information boxes include two models which can be benefited from, for our purpose, which is the improvement of the processes, and also in decision-making in terms of which processes to initiate improvements from.

Quality Function Deployment (QFD), when used in software companies, was suggested to deem the model of the software process as the customer, and the processes as the customer requirements (Richardson & Ryan, 2001).

Four Phase QFD model consists of these four matrices related to: planning for product or house of quality, deploying of parts, planning for processes, and finally, planning for production (Richardson & Ryan, 2001).

Software Process Matrix (SPM) is a model built on quality function deployment for small software companies offering an improvement strategy to them, and it encompasses processes, practices, and their relationships (Richardson, 2001).

SPM is a model developed specifically for small software companies and can be applied in similar contexts.

McKinsey framework is another tool which can address the problems and portray the gaps between the current and target situations.

Table 2.3 Tailored McKinsey 7S Table

Dimension (7S)	*Current KPI*	*Target KPI*	*Gap (Percentage)*	*Improvement Area(s)/-(IA)*	*Action Plan(s)*	*R*	*A*	*C*	*I*
				IA 1 IA 2 IA 3	Action 1 Action 2 Action 3				

McKinsey 7s Framework is a framework introduced during the 1970s by McKinsey & Co. (Channon & Caldart, 2015) which can be used for analyzing organizations and their effectiveness, considering seven factors in the examination, which are: strategy, system, structure, style, shared values, staff, and skills (Singh, 2013).

A sample McKinsey table is presented above (Table 2.3).

Another useful method is called A3 problem-solving.

A3 Problem Solving Method is a method used for problem-solving in lean thinking which takes numerous factors into consideration while analyzing a problem: history of the problem, current condition, proposal, time analysis and cost, possible implementation, and results (Kurnia, Juliantoro, Suhendra, Zy, & Apriyani, 2024).

To implement this method, the factors mentioned in the information box are included on a paper, allocating space to each factor for the answers. Visuals and statistics can be contained in the sections assigned for answers when they seem appropriate. Additionally, different templates are available on the internet which can be used for this purpose, although the main sections are almost the same.

Failure Model and Effect Analysis can also be modified for use for problem identification within the processes in software companies.

FMEA (Failure Mode and Effect Analysis) is a commonly utilized tool for risk management and also identifying potential problem areas in processes.

Its steps have been tailored for software, which can be summarized as:

- Identification of the components probable to fail in the production environment.

- Detecting and numbering the failure modes (FM).
- Identification of the effect of these FMs.
- Ranking of modes based on severity, occurrence, and detection.
- Calculation of risk priority number (RPN).
- Solving FMs from the highest RPN (Soman & Pareek, 2024).

The last method discussed here is the as-is and could-be model. As-Is and Could-Be Defect Removal Model (DRM) model was depicted for a software project in the literature, which can be of great help when implementing the model in practice (Redzic & Baik, 2006).

NOTES

Our observations shed light on the fact that after the implementation and completion of action plans, no one is going back to compare the current situation with the old situation before identifying the improvement areas and undertaking actions. Everything is considered as completed, till a manager comes and asks this question: "What benefits did these actions fetch to the company?"

Unfortunately, like everyone, managers are so much focused on the completion of the tasks that they forgot to query the improvements made.

Given all explained, to fill this gap, we have added the percentage of improvement in the last column of our As-Is and Could-Be IA CA model table to show the difference between the values before CA and after CA expressed in percentage to be both straightforward and practical (Table 2.4).

Table 2.4 As-Is and Could-Be Improvement Area (IA) Corrective Action (CA) Model

SDLC Phase	*Improvement Area Detected*	*Importance (High, Medium, Low)*	*Metric*	*As-Is Value*	*Could-Be Value*	*CA Planned*	*Value after CA*	*Percentage of Improvement*
Phase 1	IA 1	High						
Phase 2	IA 2	Medium						

NOTES

Finding the problems and determining the improvement areas is not an easy task. Apart from all the tools, methods, and techniques, it requires skills, knowledge, and experience. If you don't have experience, then you can gain it by discussing the matters with others and asking for their comments and opinions.

Some important issues related to the concepts in this chapter are:

- *Don't try to build and create a tool from scratch. First, search for the existing ones. Tailoring and modification are options themselves.*
- *Lots of tools we use today originate from the tools designed for manufacturing. Therefore, search for tools in other contexts. They can be redesigned accordingly!*
- *Articles are available regarding the causes of problems within software companies. Reading them before initiating your work provides you with an extra insight which simplifies the whole process of detection of causes and categorization of them.*
- *Comparing the results from your analysis with the findings of the related articles can work as a double-checking mechanism.*

In line with the aforementioned notes, it is good to take a look at diverse classes of problems dealt with in software projects.

Classification of Software Projects' Causes of Problems was performed by categorizing the causes under four classes of: people tasks, methods, and environment. Each of these "classes" is then, detailed into various "types" in accordance with the problem's cause, for instance, customers as a "type" is part of the "class of environment" (Lehtinen & Mantyla, 2011).

Finally, it is worth taking a look at what methods are labeled as basic quality control tools and can be benefited from in diagnosing the problems.

Seven Basic Quality Control (QC) Tools adopted for problem identification include:

- process flowcharting,
- cause-and-effect analysis,

- Pareto analysis,
- histograms,
- check sheets or tally sheets,
- scatter diagrams, and
- control charts (Herbert et al., 2003).

References

Card, A. J. (2016). The Problem with '5 whys'. *BMJ Quality & Safety*, 26, 1–7.

Channon, D. F., & Caldart, A. A. (2015). McKinsey 7S Model†. In C. L. Cooper, J. McGee, & T. Sammut-Bonnici, *Wiley Encyclopedia of Management*. https://doi.org/10.1002/9781118785317.weom120005

Daft, R. L. (2008). *Organization Theory*. Mason, OH: South-Western Cengage Learni.

Damele, G., Bazzana, G., Andreis, F., Aquilio, F., Arnoldi, S., & Pessi, E. (1996). Process Improvement through Root Cause Analysis. In S. B. Bologna, *Achieving Quality in Software* (pp. 35–47). Boston: Springer.

Francis, P., Leon, D., Minch, M., & Podgurski, A. (2004). Tree-Based Methods for Classifying Software Failures. *Proceedings of the 15th International Symposium on Software Reliability Engineering (ISSRE'04)* (pp. 451–462). Saint-Malo, France: 15th International Symposium on Software Reliability Engineering (ISSRE'04).

Hasan, Z., & Hossain, M. S. (2018). Improvement of Effectiveness by Applying PDCA Cycle or Kaizen: An Experimental Study on Engineering Students. *Journal of Scientific Research*, 10(2), 159–173.

Herbert, D., Curry, A., & Angel, L. (2003). Use of Quality Tools and Techniques in Services. *The Service Industries Journal*, 23(4), 61–80.

Karuppusami, G., & Gandhinathan, R. (2006). Pareto Analysis of Critical Success Factors in Total Quality Management: A Literature Review and Analysis. *The TQM Magazine*, 18(4), 372–385.

Kurnia, H., Juliantoro, K. B., Suhendra, Zy, A. T., & Apriyani. (2024). Combination of Lean Thinking and A3 Problem-Solving Methods to Reduce the Cost of Purchasing Cleaning Agents in a Paint Manufacturer in Indonesia. *SINERGI*, 28(1), 103–114.

Lehtinen, T. O., & Mantyla, M. V. (2011). What Are Problem Causes of Software Projects?; Data of Root Cause Analysis at Four Software Companies. *2011 International Symposium on Empirical Software Engineering and Measurement* (pp. 388–391). Alberta, Canada: IEEE.

Mintzberg, H. (1980). Structure in 5's: A Synthesis of the Research on Organization Design. *Management Science*, 26(3), 322–341.

Ohno, T. (1988). *Toyota Production System: Beyond Large-Scale Production*. New York: Productivity Press.

Pansara, R. R. (2023). Cultivating Data Quality to Strategies, Challenges, and Impact on Decision-Making. *International Journal of Management Education for Sustainable Development*, 6(6), 24–33.

Pargaonkar, S. (2022). *International Journal of Science and Research (IJSR)*. Defect Management and Root Cause Analysis: Pillars of Excellence in Software Quality Engineering, 12(9), 53–55.

Redzic, C., & Baik, J. (2006). Six Sigma Approach in Software Quality Improvement. *Proceedings of the Fourth International Conference on Software Engineering Research Management and Applications (SERA'06)* (pp. 396–406). Saettle: Fourth International Conference on Software Engineering Research.

Richardson, I. (2001). Software Process Matrix: A Small Company SPI Model. *Software Process Improvement and Practice*, 6(3), 157–165.

Richardson, I., & Ryan, K. (2001). Software Process Improvements in a Very Small Company. Software Quality Professional, 3(2), 23–35.

Sakdiyah, S. H., Eltivia, N., & Afandi, A. (2022). Root Cause Analysis Using Fishbone Diagram: Company. *Journal of Applied Business, Taxation and Economics Research (JABTER)*, 1(6), 566–576.

Sanches, C., De Sordi, J. O., Ferreira Junior, S., Meireles, M., & Da Silva, O. R. (2015). Comparative Study of the Causal Matrix and Causal Determinant. *Total Quality Management*, 26(9–10), 1095–1112.

Singer, J., Sim, S. E., & Lethbridge, T. C. (2008). Software Engineering Data Collection for Field Studies. In F. Shull, J. Singer, & D. I. Sjøberg, *Guide to Advanced Empirical Software Engineering* (pp. 9–34). London: Springer.

Singh, A. (2013). A Study of Role of McKinsey's 7S Framework in Achieving Organizational Excellence. *Organization Development Journal*, 31(3), 39–51.

Soman, S., & Pareek, P. K. (2024). An Empirical Study to Identify and Weigh Risk Attributes through the Application of FMEA in the Software Industry: Focus on MSME and SME IT Firms in the Bengaluru Region. *ASEAN Engineering Journal*, 14(1), 223–227.

Chapter 3

Strategy

3.1 Introduction

Let us begin this chapter by bringing the definitions of strategy first. What is widely known about the strategy is that it is related to the future.

Strategy can be interpreted as the guidelines that direct the decisions regarding and to the future (Mintzberg, 1978).

It was also defined as a means of setting organizational purposes with regards to its long-term goals, action plans, and priorities for the allocation of resources (Hax & Majluf, 1988).

Mintzberg has compiled different definitions for strategy and described them as 5Ps of: ploy, plan, pattern, perspective, and position (Mintzberg, 1987).

NOTES

Unfortunately, "strategy" as a word sometimes is used in the incorrect place. Decisions and plans are named wrongly as strategies even if they don't explicitly bear the characteristics of a strategy.

The issue that should not be forgotten is that the words and terms can be perceived differently when used in various contexts and by diverse people. For instance, "dynamics" meaning differs when comprehended by a system thinker and used by a quality expert when talking about the processes and

DOI: 10.4324/9781003491606-3

their relations, even if slightly. To avoid such misapprehension in a software company, quality experts can take the following initiatives:

- *Preparing an internal glossary for the company.*
- *Compiling terms and words for each department and making it available to everyone.*
- *Designing the corporate templates including the jargon section at the beginning of each document.*

An initiative that software companies can take in order to standardize their usage of terms can be leveraging AI in developing chatbots or AI-based solutions assisting the users with the right comprehension of related jargon.

In some of the studies, the distinction between strategy and strategy formation was stressed.

Strategy formation has been tried to be formulated into different steps. The forces playing a role in shaping the strategies were stated to be: environment, organizational operating system or bureaucracy, and leadership, which has a mediating role between the first two forces (Mintzberg, 1978).

Strategy formation was said to be dependent on a company's unique situation, strategic goals, style of management, administrative culture, and organizational culture (Hax & Majluf, 1988).

NOTES

While guiding teams and individuals as part of management consultancy, the best example that can be come up with is to resemble the strategist or the strategy team in a company, which is responsible for helping with pivoting around the helm, observing the conditions to avoid any collisions with rocks or any objects, and being aware of the high waves causing capsizing, briefly the first and second mates, if considering the CEO as the captain.

Strategists are the navigators of a company, while tools work as their compass, and strategies are the actions taken to reach the destination. Their responsibility becomes harder and harder as the company's size becomes bigger. The employment and the career life of the employees will be excessively dependent on their decisions. They can lead the ship to the harbor despite the difficulties that might arise during the journey, or they may fail to fulfill their duties, which will then result in the resizing of the company or the complete closure of the company.

Many companies have apprehended the significance of having an insightful and knowledgeable team of strategists, and what is observed is that the strategists move between rival companies from time to time, called "poaching." There may be some debate on how ethical is this practice; nevertheless, it does not stop the companies from saving themselves by applying to this method.

The other side is the strategists themselves. You might have heard that the new chief has brought his team to the company many times. Individual strategists have started to build networks with those with whom they can work and go on well, and they have formed their very own team. They may resign from a company at the same time or with little time variance from each other and then join another company as a team. The companies, in such situations, may not have much choice, since they are after success and they are ready to pay what it takes, mostly.

Strategy formation can be done through different approaches.

Bottom-Up Approach is a strategy formation process where top management just sets directions, without determining actions and details for operational decisions at different levels of the organization (Kim et al., 2014).

Top-Down Approach is another strategy formation process, as implied from its name, when the strategies are coming from the top management and it is broken into actions with details as it reache the levels at the bottom.

Initial results will be then taken into consideration by the top management to alter the plans (Kim et al., 2014).

NOTES

The choice of the approach may be dependent on several factors. The prominent factor is whether the employees are ready for a bottom-up approach or not.

In practice, many companies prefer the top-down approach and employees at all levels of the organization receive the guide on what they should do. The incontrovertible benefit is that they cannot claim that they did not have any idea of what to do when it comes to the performance evaluation.

In the contrary, the bottom-up approach seems much more compliant with today's concepts of employee engagement and empowerment. Employees are involved in the process of strategy formation and their opinions, idea, experience, and insights are encouraged and expected to be shared. Some of the drawbacks of applying this approach might be the following:

- *The need for extra efforts to coordinate the strategies coming from different departments.*
- *Failure in alignment of strategies across different departments.*
- *Losing sight of the environment and its components including the rivals.*
- *High risk of poor performance resulting from unproductive employees.*
- *Negligence of more strategic viewpoints due to more operational focus.*

Types of Strategies: Strategies were divided into eight types from deliberate to emergent strategies, where pure deliberate strategies are those meeting these conditions: performed intentionally in every detail; being common among all performers; and being comprehended as planned without the involvement of external forces (Mintzberg & Waters, 1985).

Difference between deliberate and emergent strategy planning was clearly shown in the literature. Deliberate strategy planning begins with data collection, is followed by rational analysis, and ends with strategy formulation, whereas the first step of emergent planning is learning and experience, and then the rational analysis takes place, and finally the strategy is formulated (Bolisani & Bratianu, 2017).

Knowing the type of strategy helps us to understand how the strategies are formed; or explicitly, "are they planned or do they emerge?" It will equip us with knowledge on how they will work in different contexts; why some strategies fail in some contexts while some do not; how to make decisions on the choice of strategy; and the approach toward strategy formation.

Organizations are also divided into diverse groups based on their strategic types.

TYPES OF ORGANIZATIONS STRATEGICALLY

Four strategic types were suggested for organizations in association with how they approach their organizational adaptation problem: defenders, analyzers, prospectors, and reactors (Miles et al., 1978).

NOTES

Let us take a deeper look at the aforementioned classification.

You may probably know the software companies that have been offering specific solutions and producing certain products, not widening the range of products and services, and have no tendency to do so. These companies will dominate a part of the market and keep on focusing on it. These are defenders. What would you think will happen to such software companies? Ignoring the trends and the advances in the environment like changes in the needs of the customers or the emergence of new solutions can put them in a fatal position.

Prospectors are like the seekers of opportunities in the software industry. They are agile and flexible in nature, and they have eyes for every potential opportunity to introduce a new product or solution to the market. They, due to the constant changes, are endangered by a low level of profitability or overuse of the resources (Miles et al., 1978).

Analyzer is the type that tries to keep its position somewhere between the previous two forms; not to be too flexible as the prospectors and not to be too defender of its current situation. The risks these types of companies face are lack of efficiency and effectiveness (Miles et al., 1978).

Reactors are the companies that fail in the previous strategies (Miles et al., 1978).

NOTES

Proactivity and reactivity are the concepts that have been used in our daily lives, specifically during recent years. The use of the terms varies by the context. Human resources are after individuals who have a proactive approach toward their work. Proactive workers are those who dare to take initiative.

Another use of the proactive notion is in quality management. Quality experts are making attempts to improve their risk management practices by implementing a proactive approach toward the risks, which exactly means not waiting for the risks to occur but taking the necessary precautions and devising plans to prevent them from turning into issues.

It is the same when it comes to strategy and the environment. Some companies tend to shape their environment, while some prefer to be watchers, and some are just the respondents. They look for any changes in the environment and react to them. These companies, if lacking the vital flexible nature and agile strategies, will encounter with critical issues at the time of changes. The cases are not few in the technology sector.

Clients are part of the environment, external to the companies. Changes in their demands, expectations, preferences, and purchasing behavior have an impact on the company. It should not be forgotten that companies are open systems; they are in exchange of resources and information with their environment and what is included inside the environment.

What we usually recommend our clients to do is to create the needs of the customers and shape the environment as they wish if they are capable, since it would not be that easy. Let us take a quick glance at famous technology companies. Most of them are not fulfilling the demands as part of their response, but meeting them after creating them!

Always keep in mind that customers might not know what they want in detail. They may just have a general view. Even if they do, their views may change over time or they can be convinced to accept a better choice if they haven't had any opinions before. Thus, getting to know your customers is one of the many keys to success for companies. It is noteworthy that the vast shifts toward an agile approach emanate from the need to focus on customers more and get them more involved throughout the production rather than solely in the final product!

McKinsey 7S model was described in the preceding chapter. The model described in the next information box bears some different and similar dimensions to McKinsey 7S.

9S Model for Strategy Implementation is the revised version of previous models like McKinsey 7s, which encompass these dimensions: structure, system, strategy, supply chain, style, set targets, shared values, synergy, and strategic performance (Twum et al., 2024).

Companies are recommended to employ 9S since it centers on managing the supply chain, defining clear goals, and promoting collaborative synergy. (Twum et al., 2024).

NOTES

Coming to practice, companies can work on the previously mentioned dimensions to implement strategies as they are intended. Let us delineate this with more details.

In a similar vein to what has been mentioned before regarding the alignment of structure with the strategy, there is a need to check on the appropriateness of the organizational structure with the strategies formulated. We have talked of organizational structure a lot, but what does it really mean?

Organizational Structure *was defined by employing three components: reporting relationships, groupings and departments, and systems to support effectiveness in communicating, harmonizing, and integrating the efforts among different departments* (Daft, 2008).

Implementation of the strategy shall be done by paying attention to the system dimension, which incorporates employees, all activities and tasks, and their coordination. All these make a system. By taking a look at the definition of a system, which is a whole comprising of elements that all work together to achieve the goal or goal(s) of the system, this dimension can be comprehended better.

Supply chain is one of the dimensions that differentiates the 9S model from the previous models. Particularly during recent years, extra awareness has been developed in this regard. The main reason might be the rising attention toward sustainability, and its emphasis on and care for the supply chain and suppliers.

Setting targets has been gaining popularity during recent decades, and companies are seeking new options to do it more correctly, comprehensively, and easily. Purchasing tools that have simplified, visualized, and automated target setting and the subsequent tracking of the progress are just part of these efforts.

Shared values play an important role in strategy implementation, although despite this critical role, it is the dimension that is usually dismissed. Building and cultivating a shared value system in a company can bring other benefits to the organization which among them organizational commitment (mentioned in Chapter 1) might take place.

Synergy stresses collaboration in a company. The need for more collaboration is just another example of many reasons for high preference and a tendency among software companies toward the agile approach. As consultants, when trying to highlight the significance of synergy, we say that the sum resulting from synergy is greater than the sum resulting from adding all individual works separately.

It is worth reviewing the literature for the factors playing a role in the success of the strategy implementation, and an invaluable insight is shared in the next information box.

Strategy Implementation is like a bridge between planned and realizing strategy, and three elements making it successful were highlighted:

- Communicating the strategy.
- Determining strategic actors, encouraging, and backing them.
- Coordinating the organizational goal-setting system and organizational structure with strategy (Aaltonen & Ikävalko, 2002).

NOTES

After reading the preceding information box, how well defined they are in consistency with what we usually observe in practice can be realized. The elements of implementing the strategy successfully are what we detect as the common lack between the software companies regarding strategy management!

Many problems are detected due to inefficient communication of strategy in companies. This may result in miscomprehension of the strategies, which leads to planning and taking incorrect actions. The critical issue here is to clearly define strategies regardless of the type of approach selected for strategy formation. We, as consultants, suggest the companies that prefer the bottom-up approach of strategy formation have a controlling mechanism for checking the correctness and appropriateness of strategies as they are formulated. This can take different forms like holding meetings inside each department and discussing them.

Another option is to prepare a guide for strategy formulation and make it accessible to employees internally, which is riskier compared to the previous option.

The third option which is usually welcomed by the employees in holding workshops in and inter departments. By doing so, the success of coordination and alignment of strategies among departments can also be enhanced. At the same time, top management can also share its plans and ideas with the employees and this clarification aids with more reasonable outcomes of the strategy formation process.

Strategic actors were the hardest among all for us to relate to, for the reason that we haven't seen any related practices in companies. After spending much time in a company, you may learn who is behind the strategies, but, even after a long time, you may rarely have any ideas of the RACI related to strategies. For these reasons, expecting encouragement and support is not meaningful in the lack of strategic actors' delegation.

The misalignment between strategy and structure is the pain point in many software companies and they mostly think of the structure as fragile, whereas in case of any slight change, structural cracks and fractures occur.

Strategy posture is one of those concepts, and many examples can be thought of after explaining it. Let us see the definition in the next information box.

Strategy Posture is about making the intention of your strategies clear, taking three forms of shaping, adapting, and reserving the right to play through investments (Courtney et al., 1997).

NOTES

You may remember the notes section where we suggested the companies to create the demand not to respond to them. This is called shaping.

Adapting is to find a way to survive and fight, other than creating new opportunities and innovating. The company will not have a tendency to shape or shake the industry, but it remains in it by making choices regarding the strategies to compete and overcome the rivals.

As in the remainder of this section, let us investigate the popular strategies.

Strategies Used in Computer Software Industry were studied in a research and five strategies were recognized with practices like building alliances, releasing versions of a current product, appealing price-to-quality ratio, market preparation, and technological superiority (Easingwood et al., 2006).

Strategies used in agile teams to increase customer value were stated as prioritization based on customer value and validation, concentration on value elements of the customer's market segment, and implementation of recent relevant agile practices (Sambinelli & Borges, 2019).

Three Generic Strategies were defined by Porter as cost leadership, focus, and differentiation; first is about keeping the cost low; the second is about choosing a segment with two choices of cost focus and differentiation focus; and the third is about offering uniqueness in different terms like products and services (Porter, 1985).

3.2 Analysis of Improvement Areas

In Chapter 2, methods were discussed for the identification of improvement areas. Improvement areas were obtained by employing diverse tools and methods. Then, what is next?

We have a list of improvement areas in our hands. What should be done in the following steps?

A company rarely possesses all the resources required to implement many improvements simultaneously. Prioritization of these improvement areas is what can be of great help at this stage. There are many prioritization techniques, like the 100-point method, weighting methods, and the Eisenhower matrix, which can be adopted for this purpose. It depends on the number of improvement areas, their dependency, the difference between their importance and urgency, preference toward a specific approach, and the skills of the expert who wants to use them.

Within the scope of strategic software quality management, these improvement areas are required to be assessed regarding their impact on the strategies of the company. To put it differently, we intend to measure how much each improvement area is important in terms of each objective and its higher level, which is strategy. To make the hierarchy clear, let us take a look at the next information box.

Pyramid of OKR Building Blocks starts from the mission at the top, followed by vision, strategy, objectives, and key results; objectives are about what we concentrate on the short term and key results point the way to understand our achievement (Niven & Lamorte, 2016).

Table 3.1 can be used for the analysis of the improvement areas from a strategic perspective.

The details that guide you to use the table are provided below.

- Improvement area column represents the improvement areas gained from the use of different methods.

Table 3.1 Strategic Prioritization of Improvement Areas

	Vision							
	Strategies(S)/ Normalized Weight	*S1/weight of S1 regarding vision*			*S2/weight of S2 regarding vision*		*Sum of weights*	*Rank*
	Objectives (O)/ Normalized Weight	*O1/weight of O1 regarding S1*	*O2/weight of O2 regarding S1*	*O3/weight of O3 regarding S1*	*O4/weight of O4 regarding S2*	*O5/weight of O5 regarding S2*		
Improvement Areas (IA)								
IA 1		Impact of IA 1 on O1	Impact of IA 1 on O2	Impact of IA 1 on O3	Impact of IA 1 on O4			
IA 2		Effect of IA 2 on O1						
IA 3		Effect of IA 3 on O1						

- The row at the top includes vision, which is in line with the hierarchy.
- The strategies row embraces all the strategies identified, and they are separated by a forward slash sign "/" from the weight assigned to it regarding the vision. It shows the impact of that specific strategy in realizing the vision. Let us express this with an example.
- Two strategies were identified. These strategies should be weighted according to their impact in terms of vision. We recommend using such a scale:
  - 0 for no impact,
  - 1 for slight impact,
  - 3 for medium impact, and
  - 5 for strong impact.

The impact assessment results are: three for S1 and five for S2. Now we need to normalize the results so that their sum will be one and the data will be easier to work with. Normalized weight for S1 will be 3 divided by 8 which is 0.375 and for S2 will be 0.625 (shown in Table 3.2).

- The objective rows include all the objectives, and they are written under the strategy they are related to. The weight is assigned by taking the impact of an objective in the realization of the strategy it is associated with. Again, normalization is done.
- O1 weight = 1, O2 weight = 3, and O3 weight = 3.
- These weights were given based on impact on S1.

Table 3.2 Example of Strategic Prioritization of Improvement Areas

	Vision							
	Strategies(S)/N. Weight	*S1/0.375*			*S2/0.625*		*Sum of weights*	*Rank*
	Objectives (O)/N. Weight	*O1/0.142*	*O2/0.428*	*O3/0.428*				
Improvement Areas (IA)								
IA 1		1	1	3				
IA 2								

- IA1 row is filled out with the same rules taking the impact of IA1 on the objectives into consideration. The impact of IA1 on vision by means of S1 is calculated by:

$$1 \times 0.142 \times 0.375 + 1 \times 0.428 \times 0.375 + 3 \times 0.428 \times 0.375 =$$
$$0.05 + 0.16 + 0.48 = 0.69$$

- Similar calculations should be done for finding the impact of IA2 on vision by means of S2. Then, the sum of these two values is calculated and added to the sum of weights column.
- At the last step, values in the sum of the weights column are compared and are ranked by numbering the highest value as 1, continuing to the least number.

3.3 Review of Different Strategic Tools and Techniques

Some strategic tools and techniques have already been discussed in the preceding chapters. In this chapter, those that have not been explained yet are introduced.

Benchmarking has been recommended for use as a strategic management tool to advance and support quality of decision making including four kinds of activities:

- competitive advantage benchmarking,
- strategies benchmarking,
- process benchmarking, and
- performance benchmarking (Prašnikar et al., 2005).

NOTES

In a similar vein with the last information box, benchmarking can be used for a wide range of activities. It is usually the first method one employs when given a task involving some kind of comparison or let us put it in a different way: "learning about how the others have done it!"

In practice, competitive advantage and strategy benchmarking are done by top management and strategists in a software company. What can be observed is that it is among the favorite tools for strategy selection and formation.

Process benchmarking can be done by comparing with the best practices within the company. Unfortunately, when searching for process benchmarking cases online, there are not many processes of other companies available. In this situation, articles, process improvement case study books, and expert insights can be used for benchmarking. Benchmarking can be against a standard, model, and framework as well. This is more applicable when benchmarking is performed for the processes.

Performance benchmarking is usually conducted by taking the financial performance into account even if performance can be compared in non-financial terms. Like what is mentioned in Chapter 1, BSC is a tool that considers three other dimensions: customer, internal business processes, and innovation and growth, together with a financial perspective to balance the approach toward performance.

Porter's Five Competitive Forces Model encapsulates the forces playing a role in strategy formation of which their analysis assists with understanding the industry's competition and profitability: the threat of entrants together with the threat of alternative products and/or services, and bargaining power of suppliers and buyers (Porter, 2008).

NOTES

Number of software companies established every day might not be as high as the number of software products introduced to the market daily. Even the children can code now and they can release their own games and applications on different platforms. Alternative products endanger companies to the point that many start-up businesses fail in the first years of their activities.

The other problem is that buyers have gained bargaining power due to the vast number of similar products. They can change their suppliers so easily just by a click, for instance.

Imitation is another problem in the market. You may introduce a different product or service, trying to leverage this uniqueness; however, the high speed of imitation results in the emergence of rivals. The competition is to the extent that adding a technically simple feature, such as making the user interface friendlier or even having a better marketing strategy, for instance, having a famous social media influencer using your product or service can lead to outperforming your rivals and winning their customers as well.

To sum up, given all that was discussed, several issues should be noticed:

- *Try to know your customers well.*
- *Do not underestimate the design. Nowadays, we observe very simple technologies with lots of alternatives that win the race because of their minimal design.*
- *Take time and plan for an almost perfect marketing strategy! Sometimes, or even most of the times it is about:*
  - *How you present your product or service,*
  - *How deep is the impression on the customers,*
  - *And how this relationship is maintained throughout the time making the customers committed to your products or services; the reason behind the huge budgets allocated to customer relationship management (CRM).*

Talking of marketing, let us take a glance at the concept of strategic market management.

Strategic Market Management involves internal and external analysis; external analysis consists of four sections, which are customer, competitor, market, and environmental analysis, whereas internal analysis incorporates performance analysis and identification of strategy-influencing factors (Aaker, 2001).

Next comes one of the techniques preferred by companies with a more scientific approach, seeking for more precise results.

Goal Question Metric (GQM) is an approach covering three levels of conceptual, operational, and quantitative corresponding to goal, question, and metric, respectively, building a hierarchical structure with goals at the top breaking down into questions and metrics successively (Basili et al., 1994).

NOTES

GQM has been adopted by many software companies for a long time. It is a simple but at the same time comprehensive method starting from defining goals, then writing questions for each goal and next, specifying metrics for each question. The hierarchical view of the mode aids a clear understanding of the concepts.

Scenario Planning, which can be deemed as a strategy tool, is concerned with creating diverse scenarios regarding the future of a company together with the relevant strategies that equip managers with a framework to develop strategies and plans (Verity, 2003).

NOTES

Despite the usefulness of scenario planning, especially by generating novel scenarios and paying attention to hidden points regarding the future, it is not employed a lot in practice. It might be due to its qualitative nature since software companies are much after quantifiable concepts.

Strategic Pyramid was proposed for implementing strategies in a company, facilitating its transformations from as-is to to-be state by coordinating strategies and its breakdown into operational tasks (Teixeira & Pereira, 2015).

The bottom of the pyramid includes people, processes, and systems, followed by KPIs (Teixeira & Pereira, 2015).

3.4 Determination of the Appropriate Strategic Tools and Techniques

To determine the suitable appropriate tools and techniques, the first step is to specify your purpose; "what is your purpose of using strategic tools and techniques?" The answers can be categorized under one of these categories:

- Strategy research.
- Strategy selection and/or formation.
- Strategic alignment and coordination.
- Strategy communication.
- Strategy implementation.
- Strategy performance evaluation.

These groups are consistent with the steps a company should take to manage its strategies. Let us delineate these groups one by one first and then discuss the steps that should be taken for strategic management.

The first group of tools helps with identifying the existing strategies. This can include methods like strategic benchmarking or SWOT analysis.

The second group is related to the tools and methods for strategy selection. If you have a list of potential strategies, you can employ an MCDM method to prioritize them and find the one most appropriate in terms of the specified criteria. Strategy formation may be done according to a top-down or bottom-up approach, and the tools for this process should be selected taking the applied approach into consideration.

Strategy alignment and coordination is about two different types of tools: the tools to harmonize the actions within the company and the tools to get aligned with the strategies in terms of factors like resources, structure, processes, and procedures.

Strategy communication tools are those tools informing the employees of the strategies and the actions they are supposed to perform to contribute to them. The OKR method is one of them, which, by defining objectives and key results, draw a clear path to the strategies for the employees at different levels of the organization.

Strategy implementation tools assist managers in having strategies implemented in a comprehensive and systematic way, like a strategic pyramid.

Strategy performance evaluation tools are those that aid in controlling and monitoring the performance such as KPIs.

The remainder of this section elaborates on the steps from conducting research on the strategy to the performance evaluation.

At the first step, it is better to search for the cases and instances as many as possible. Check for the strategies created by software companies nationally and internationally. At the same time, try to define the factors that play a role in their choice of strategy. You can benefit from system dynamics and draw flow. The question that might be raised here is how to narrow down the scope of the research.

First, begin with looking for recent cases. The world is changing fast, and so is the context for the strategies. It is better to find examples of the closest context in terms of time.

The second option is to list factors that might affect your strategy selection and seek the literature for similar situations. For instance, one of the factors is uncertainty. Check for strategies under low or high uncertainty conditions. The other might be the size of the company. This can play an important role since the strategies implemented by small and large companies vary.

The third option is that if your company is part of a network or an economic agglomeration like an industrial cluster, review and examine the strategies of other companies in the same agglomeration. It will aid a lot with understanding the environment as part of the environment is shared and common between such companies.

The second step is to select a strategy or strategies from the available list obtained from the first step and/or combine and integrate them with the strategies that are formulated newly. Based on the strategy formation approaches, bottom-up and top-down approaches, the actions take place at these steps differ accordingly.

Your strategy may be selected as differentiation. It is one of the well-known strategies that works well today even in the more dynamic and turbulent nature of the environment. This category of strategies covers a wide range. It can be a unique way to support your customers; it can be a feature adding to your product. During and after strategy formation, some practices can be of great assistance:

- Define the scope of the strategy in terms of the department(s) who will be mainly involved. In the previous examples, the CRM team and the designing team will be those. Work closely with them and also with your marketing team.
- Scenario planning is a tool that can portray the future situation. This can be done by defining three scenarios as realistic, pessimistic, and optimistic. It is of help in having an idea of how things will go in the best and worst conditions. They will be the answers to these questions of the top managers and strategists:
- What if it goes well?
- What if it doesn't work?
- What if it goes as planned?

The **third step** is strategic alignment and coordination. This step encompasses the practices to coordinate the strategies and actions across different departments. Alignment of structure with the strategy is another critical issue here.

Strategy communication is the **fourth**. There are some critical issues here worth noticing:

- Devise a two-way communication system to support the feedback flow.
- Communicate the visions and strategies to external stakeholders as well.

One study turns our attention toward the external role of communication and clarifies it with an example that having good relationships with stakeholders is of importance since their support or disagreement may have an impact on the achievement of organizational goals (Moss & Warnaby, 1998).

NOTES

Observation and experience point to a similar outcome with the academic papers. Strategy communication in software companies is the step that is skipped in many cases or performed at an insufficient level. Sometimes, communication is just perceived as sending a short formal email. We must consider the effectiveness of the communication channel we choose in the context and for the purpose it is picked up for.

In addition, communication with external stakeholders is usually ignored. Although some companies already have their own successful ways for this, others miss this step since they believe that the external stakeholders do not value the strategies at all, but solely their outcomes.

Strategy implementation is the **fifth step**, and we may say the hardest part. At the end of the first two steps, the right strategies have been formulated, but all these efforts will not lead to their destination if strategies are not performed as planned.

NOTES

From time to time, we observe such a situation in software companies when one or two departments have interpreted the strategies not as they were meant to and therefore, their actions have deviated from the intended path, not supporting the strategies. This is not a desired situation, nevertheless, it can be fixed. It is the prominent reason why we talked of having controlling mechanisms and underlined checking for the initial outcomes with the aim to prevent the occurrence and recurrence of such cases. The negative outcome depends on the department, its size, the scope of its contribution to the strategies, and its involvement level in the strategy realization. We set this example for our customers. Imagine you are driving your car and at a junction, you were offered two options. You continue driving, but after some time, it turned out that it is the wrong choice. You may make a U-turn to go back to the junction. Which situation seems better among these two?

- *Having driven for 2 hours, 100 kilometers, and then realizing the problem.*
- *Having driven for half an hour, 25 kilometers, and then understanding the problem.*

Apart from the time spent, the cost and effort it took should not be underestimated. Within our example, you, as the driver, drove for 2 hours. Is the effort, your energy, and your level of tiredness the same as in the other scenario? Not, of course. As for cost, what about the fuel you have purchased? Using fuel for two hours on a wrong route will put you in the need of extra fuel sooner.

To sum it up, reviewing the initial outcomes is the best way to avoid problems, and the sooner the problem is identified and fixed, the less will be the loss in terms of time, cost, and effort.

The **last step** is the evaluation of the strategic performance.

Effectiveness of Strategic Performance Evaluation System is influenced by numerous factors: the criteria, their weights or priorities, the evaluation process, and the definitions of the criteria (Saad, 2001).

These systems should be able to:

- measure operating control systems along with strategic ones,
- direct focus toward the critical processes, and
- translation of strategies to actions (Saad, 2001).

Return on investment (ROI) and its related metric, return on sales (ROS), have been used to measure strategic performance across firms or over time (Banker et al., 1996).

Findings of another research regarding strategic performance measurement (SPF) (Micheli & Manzoni, 2010) can be considered as inspirations and the following suggestions can be made:

- Determine the level of measurement: measuring at a strategic level, operational level, or both.
- Specify the approach: descriptive or prescriptive.
- Determine the approach of reactions: constructive or destructive.
- Have documented procedure for performance evaluation and its preceding and succeeding processes with their details included.

NOTES

Our recommendation is to implement an integrated measurement both at the strategic and operational levels. The justification is that these strategies are broken into operational tasks at lower levels of the organizations and the outcome from the execution of these tasks then, in return, affects the strategies, resulting in their modification or alteration. This is in agreement with the loop proposed in the literature depicting an integrated performance evaluation system (Saad, 2001).

Some evaluations, or maybe we can say, most of the evaluations bear a descriptive approach, describing the current situation. They do not go beyond this border, beyond depicting the situation. One curious, or rather courageous, person may come forward and ask, "so what?"

By combining descriptive and prescriptive approaches, we can paint a picture or pictures of the future based on the outputs of the evaluation. This is only when all these efforts become meaningful. It is noteworthy that sometimes what is requested is a descriptive approach just to capture a snapshot of the situation. It may be for many reasons but frequently encountered reason is for learning about the situation and its changes in response to a change.

The next matter is what would the company do after gaining the results of the evaluation. The first thought that comes to mind is downsizing the company, unfortunately. It is important to have a constructive approach after the evaluation. For instance, instead of blaming, try learning the reasons why. Instead of accusing, try to find solutions. Managers of the software companies are sometimes so drowned in the problem itself that they cannot come out for a second, take a deep fresh breath, and see that there is a ship nearby! We highly recommend not to concentrate on accusing your people and losing time fighting and having to fight back, instead focus on the solution and ask and encourage your employees to do so.

The last notion is having documentation for evaluation entailing the details like:

- *Who is in charge of evaluation?*
- *Who is evaluated?*
- *Which departments are included in the process?*
- *What is the standardized process to ensure the employees of a fair approach?*
- *What will happen in different scenarios of the outcome? Will there be sanctions? Will there be incentives?*

References

Aaker, D. A. (2001). *Developing Business Strategies.* New York: John Wiley & Sons, Inc.

Aaltonen, P., & Ikävalko, H. (2002). Implementing Strategies Successfully. *Integrated Manufacturing Systems*, 13(6), 415–418.

Banker, R. D., CHANG, H. H., & Majumdar, S. K. (1996). A Framework for Analyzing Changes in Strategic performance. *Strategic Management Journal*, 17(9), 693–712.

Basili, V. R., Caldiera, G., & Rombach, H. D. (1994). The Goal Question Metric (GQM) Approach. Computer Science, 1–10.

Bolisani, E., & Bratianu, C. (2017). Knowledge Strategy Planning: An Integrated Approach to Manage Uncertainty, Turbulence, and Dynamics. *Journal of Knowledge Management*, 21(2), 233–253.

Courtney, H., Kirkland, J., & Viguerie, P. (1997). Strategy under Uncertainty. *Harvard Business Review*, 75(6), 1–15.

Daft, R. L. (2008). *Organization Theory.* Mason, OH: South-Western Cengage Learni.

Easingwood, C., Moxey, S., & Capleton, H. (2006). Bringing High Technology to Market: Successful Strategies Employed in the Worldwide Software Industry. *Journal of Product Innovation Management*, 23(6), 498–511.

Hax, A. C., & Majluf, N. S. (1988). The Concept of Strategy and the Strategy Formation Process. *Interfaces*, 18(3), 99–109.

Kim, Y. H., Sting, F. J., & Loch, C. H. (2014). Top-Down, Bottom-Up, or Both? Toward an Integrative Perspective on Operations Strategy Formation. *Journal of Operations Management*, 32(7–8), 462–474.

Micheli, P., & Manzoni, J.-F. (2010). Strategic Performance Measurement: Benefits, Limitations and Paradoxes. *Long Range Planning*, 43(4), 465–476.

Miles, R. E., Snow, C. C., Meyer, A. D., & Coleman, J. H. (1978). Organizational Strategy, Structure, and Process. *Academy of Management*, 3(3), 546–562.

Mintzberg, H. (1987). The Strategy Concept I: Five Ps for Strategy. *California Management Review*, 30(1), 11–24.

Mintzberg, H. (1978). Patterns in Strategy Formation. *Management Science*, 24(9), 934–948.

Mintzberg, H., & Waters, J. A. (1985). Of Strategies, Deliberate and Emergent. *Strategic Management Journal*, 6(3), 257–272.

Moss, D., & Warnaby, G. (1998). Communications Strategy? Strategy Communication? Integrating Different Perspectives. *Journal of Marketing Communications*, 4(3), 131–140.

Niven, P. R., & Lamorte, B. (2016). *Objectives and Key Results: Driving Focus, Alignment, and Engagement with OKRs.* New Jersey: Wiley.

Porter, M. E. (1985). *Competitive Advantage: Creating and Sustaining Superior Performance.* New York: Free Press.

Porter, M. E. (2008). The Five Competitive Forces That Shape Strategy. *Harvard Business Review*, 86(1), 78–93.

Prašnikar, J., Debeljak, Ž., & Ahčan, A. (2005). Benchmarking as a Tool of Strategic Management. *Total Quality Management & Business Excellence*, 16(2), 257–275.
Saad, G. H. (2001). Strategic Performance Evaluation: Descriptive and Prescriptive Analysis. *Industrial Management & Data Systems*, 101(8), 390–399.
Sambinelli, F., & Borges, M. A. (2019). Survey on Strategies to Increase Customer Value in Brazilian Agile Software Development Companies. *2019 14th Iberian Conference on Information Systems and Technologies (CISTI)* (pp. 1–7). Coimbra, Portugal: IEEE.
Teixeira, C. S., & Pereira, L. L. (2015). Pereira Diamond: Benefits Management Framework. *The International Journal of Business & Management*, 3, 47–56.
Twum, F. O., Badu, Y. A., & Boateng, P. A. (2024). The Nine "S" Model for Strategy Implementation: A Review. *Pan-African Journal of Education and Social Sciences*, 5(1), 18–27.
Verity, J. (2003). Scenario Planning as a Strategy Tool. *European Business Journal*, 5(4), 185–195.

Chapter 4

Progress Tracking

4.1 Defining the Progress Indicators

Till now we have talked about KPIs and OKRs. KPIs related to different phases of SDLC can be gained after a search on the internet and many resources are available discussing them.

In this section, we want to attract your attention toward the concepts underlying these. We will not suggest using specific KPIs or other indicators; however, we explain the logic behind defining the suitable progress indicator. Therefore, the reader will be equipped with the information which will be of help whenever progress indicators are being determined.

Let us begin with some triggering questions:

- What is progress in the context of tasks in a software company?
- What is its different status?
- What needs to be tracked in terms of its progress in a software company?

These questions lead to the next model, which we named as measurable elements related to a software company.

Let us begin with the processes.

Processes can be measured by means of KPIs. Besides, they can be measured according to their compliance with a model, framework, or standard, their effectiveness, efficiency, duration, and so on.

The variables that can be measured associated with the **employees** can vary a lot like employee performance, employee job satisfaction, number of female employees, rate of turnover, and number of organic

DOI: 10.4324/9781003491606-4

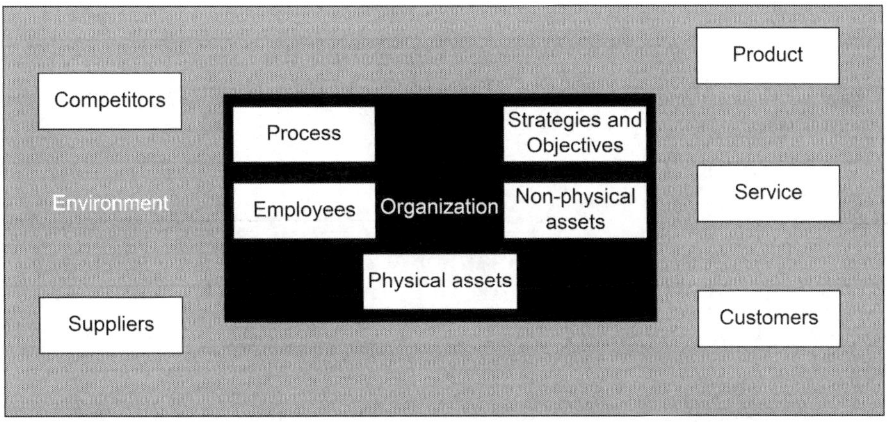

Figure 4.1 Measurable elements related to a software company.

hires in a year (shown in Figure 4.1). Some reporting frameworks suggest their metrics, which are employed globally in wide scope.

NOTES

Sustainability practices in software companies bear differences from the manufacturing firms and the social dimension is the underscored dimension in their context.

When taking of social dimension, employees first come to our mind. It is right. Different sustainability assessment organizations and authorities ask the applicants to provide information on different aspects regarding their employees. This information covers a wide range and has its own metrics precisely defined.

Similarly, there are companies and authorities assessing the human resource practices in companies with the purpose of endorsing them. In such cases, information concerning the employees is examined again, for instance, their job satisfaction, their level of work engagement, and so on.

What can be measured regarding the **physical assets** of a software company may include: the number of specific hardware; the number of purchases of a specific object in a year; and the number of laptops that have become obsolete or fixed in a year.

Nonphysical assets incorporate software development tools and software solutions. Software metrics are the main outcome of measurement related to this group.

Strategies and objectives can be measured in terms of their effectiveness and their realization. Traditionally, the financial aspects of strategies were measured by calculating ROI, for example.

Some measurable aspects of the **Product** may be quality attributes like usability, reliability, or other aspects such as cost and performance.

Service can be evaluated based on response time, or resolution time, for example.

Some measurable aspects related to **customers** may incorporate their satisfaction, net promoter score (NPS), and frequency of purchase.

Competitor is the inevitable element when your perspective is strategic, and for instance, when you analyze your competitor or benchmark, you measure aspects of them. At the first place comes their market share.

Supplier and their evaluation are gaining more and more attention as a result of the widespread global inclination toward sustainability practices. Sustainability assessments have been conducted by companies in the process of selecting their suppliers, taking into consideration aspects like the quality of their products, the price of their products, or the service they offer. From a sustainability point of view, their sustainability initiatives, or their carbon emissions within different scopes, may be measured.

In order to summarize and visualize the steps for defining the progress indicator, the flow in the coming next can be used.

The flow begins with choosing the element you want to assess. You may gain insight from Figure 4.1. Then, you are required to specify the aspects you intend to measure in association with that element. The explanations earlier can guide you through this. Suitable metrics for those aspects should be researched and then identified together with the right unit. The last step is to review all the previous steps and check for probable mistakes or the issues overlooked. Finally, the progress indicators can be identified (shown in Figure 4.2).

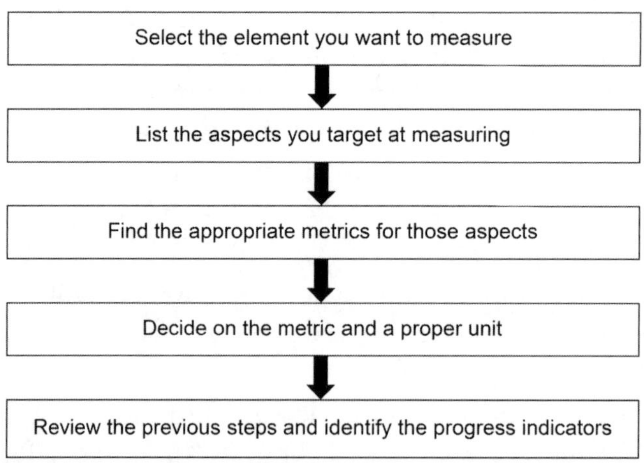

Figure 4.2 Steps for progress indicator identification.

4.2 Tracking the Progress

When asking a project manager how they track the progress, the first answer they come up with is using work breakdown structure (WBS) and Gantt chart.

Gantt Chart is a popular management tool for activity planning shaped by breaking activities into tasks, deciding on the length of activity and whether it is performed simultaneously with other tasks (Ramachandran & Karthick, 2019) or different dependencies:

- FS: Finish to start.
- SF: Start to finish.
- FF: Finish to finish.
- SS: Start to start.

WBS is essential for decomposing a project into its component activities where activities are then categorized into operations, tasks, and functions (Zecheru & Olaru, 2016).

Within the agile approach, popular tools differ a bit. They are burn down chart, burn up chart, and the notion of velocity.

Burn Up Chart depicts how much work has been completed compared to the total work that is required to be done, illuminating the overall progress.

Burn Down Chart shows how much work is remaining in comparison with the total work.

Velocity is a frequently utilized metric in agile practices, which is the amount of work completed in a sprint (short development cycle) (Pomar et al., 2014).

NOTES

As more and more software companies adopt the agile approach for their projects, the tools for tracking the progress of agile projects are becoming increasingly popular.

The other options, which were more popular before and still work when details are needed, maybe: the number of "to do" tasks; the number of tasks "in progress"; the number of tasks "done"; and the time between the creation of the task and its completion.

Since most software companies are using software tools for tracking their progress, such results and charts can be easily produced and obtained. Nonetheless, the critical point here is to have a standardization backed by a formal documentation on what "in progress" means or what "done" means in different cases. To clarify it, what I might see as done would be not considered as done by other users.

Control charts are more detailed and statistical methods to use.

Control Chart is a great tool for statistical process control, noted to be introduced by Shewhart (Chang & Tong, 2013; Shewhart, 1926) that detects two types of sources of variations in the processes: common-cause and specific-cause, in which the former is shown by a pattern over time, whereas the latter is about abrupt or unusual changes shaping events that are not associated with the normal processes (Chang & Tong, 2013).

4.3 Comparing and Reporting the Progress throughout Time

What we mean by comparing here is comparing the data driven at different points in time. For instance, we have data from 6 months ago and the data that collected last week. What are the points that should be paid attention to during comparison?

- Is the context from where the data collected the same? If the answer is yes, what are the causes of the changes? Do these changes affect the values?
- Are the values as predicted/planned? If the answer is yes, then what are the probable reasons underlying the difference?
- Looking at the values across time:
  - What went well? What do you think about the probable reasons?
  - What went wrong? Any ideas on probable reasons?
  - What went the same as before with no changes? Any probable reasons?
- Were the data collected represented in the same units?
- Was the collection method the same?
- Was the data collector the same? If not, can he/she leave some kind of impact on the data?

- Were the attendants the same? If not, can factors related to them, for instance, the department they are working at, have effects on the values and the results?
- Was the data collection tool the same? For example, if a questionnaire was used, was there a rewording of questions or reordering the questions?

Preparing reports begins with knowing your audience and the purpose for reporting. Imagine a medical doctor trying to give a talk. When he/she is in a scientific conference, the reports prepared for that case can be more complicated and they include medical terms. But what about the same doctor speaking to a group of engineers about the importance of physical activity on their well-being? Of course, the nature of reports will be less scientific in terms of the medical concepts and fewer medical terms will be incorporated in the reports. Thus, the paramount importance of knowing your audience and the purpose of the report should not be underestimated.

The following framework can help you clarify the concepts required to be reported, and visuals can be then illustrated accordingly. This framework was designed in line with the questions stated earlier shown in Table 4.1.

Table 4.1 Analysis and Comparison of Values in Reports Framework

Measurable element	
Aspect measured	
Metric used	
Unit	
Date of previous report	
Value in previous report	
Value for current period	
Types of change detected (decrease, increase, no change)	
Type of change predicted	
Probable reasons for "the difference between actual results and predictions" or "for the stability"	
Ideal or target value	
Action plans	
Start data of corrective action	
End date of corrective action	

As it is seen in the framework and as you have experience in practice, analyzing reports and coming to findings may also point at some improvement areas. Either the differences and similarities between the two values of the same variable can refer to a problem; thus, the final part of any report or presentation of the analysis should be accompanied by determining the actions required to be done for solving the problems and improving the situation; otherwise, the purpose of the analysis and reporting is not fulfilled and the matter will remain unresolved.

References

Chang, C.-W., & Tong, L.-I. (2013). Monitoring the Software Development Process Using a Short-Run Control Chart. *Software Quality Journal*, 21, 479–499.

Pomar, F. A., Calvo-Manzano, J. A., Caballero, E., & Arcilla-Cobián, M. (2014). Understanding Sprint Velocity Fluctuations for Improved Project. *Journal of Software: Evolution and Process*, 26(9), 776–783.

Ramachandran, K. K., & Karthick, K. K. (2019). Gantt Chart: An Important Tool of Management. *International Journal of Innovative Technology and Exploring Engineering*, 8(7), 140–142.

Shewhart, W. A. (1926). Quality Control Charts. *Shewhart, W. A.*, 5(4), 593–603.

Zecheru, V., & Olaru, B. G. (2016). Work Breakdown Structure (WBS) in Project Management. *Review of International Comparative Management*, 17(1), 61–69.

Chapter 5

Sustainable Continuous Improvement

5.1 Continuous Improvement

We may begin this chapter by providing a definition for continuous improvement (CI) first.

CI methods like Six Sigma, lean manufacturing, and BSC were founded on process or/and quality improvement concepts with the aim of minimizing waste, streamlining production processes, and improving quality, requiring collaboration to make improvements without the need for vast investment of capital (Bhuiyan & Baghel, 2005).

CI was mentioned as a philosophy that points to the fact that continuous attention and learning are essential in achieving excellence in marketing, production, and engineering (Terney & Anderson, 1989).

A model which was developed in a study is described in the next information box, which helps a lot with clarifying the CI-related concepts.

CI Model comprises of three groups: drivers, enablers, and results where the former group encompasses management, focus on stakeholders, performance evaluation and feedback, and learning; they are activated by innovation culture, employee focus, and detection of critical processes, standardization, and CI dissemination (Kaye & Anderson, 1999).

DOI: 10.4324/9781003491606-5

NOTES

Our observations are in consisten with the CI model brought earlier. We have experienced cases where CIs are expected from the employees, but there is no management practice implemented, and they call it "employee empowerment!" Leaving everything to the employee should not be considered as empowerment. There should be an authority to manage the tasks, track the progress, follow the activities, and coordinate the tasks between the teams and departments.

Stakeholders used to be ignored more; however, with the popularity of sustainability practices, they are now more involved in the processes since their involvement and engagement are directly questioned. The primary issue with the concept of stakeholders is that it encompasses many distinct individuals and groups and this makes it hard for the companies to identify them. Reviewing the matters related to the stakeholders under the two categories of internal and external stakeholders can be greatly advantageous in illuminating the concept.

The importance of performance evaluation and having a two-way communication (feedback mechanism) was underscored in the previous chapters. The issue here is the purpose of the evaluation: evaluate to criticize and become disappointed in your people or evaluate to improve and motivate them.

The purpose of the evaluation should clearly be communicated with the employees and the related documents should be prepared and be available for reference by the employees. If the employees perceive the evaluation as something like the first scenario (destructive), and unsure or concerned about the consequences of the evaluation, we might admit that starting from that moment, you, as the manager, will be less likely to receive data void of manipulation and falsification! You, as the manager, do not have the time and energy to collect data from operations and activities. Therefore, do not underestimate the impact of two-way effective communication in your organization, and do not ignore the importance of communicating the purpose of every action taken, in which your employees are involved. Through clear communication, make them trust you, and then you can trust the data handed to you!

Examining the organizational culture, we can say that there is a long way to go in terms of practice. Despite having academicians study the concept many times during the years, we can still feel the insufficiency concerning the concentration on the organizational culture and initiatives taken towards cultivating it in the companies.

Focusing on employees has gained more and more attention during recent years and it has become like a race for software companies to get an endorsement from different organizations and authorities in association with the practices and initiatives concerning employees. It is also used by software companies as a means of attracting talent, or, we can say, headhunting. You may remember when we mentioned that there are many human resources, but few skilled ones. This is the case. Companies compete with each other to offer the best options and opportunities to employees so that they can have the human resources with the potential of becoming a competitive advantage for a company. There is a saying in the labor market that "every employee is substitutable!" that makes it lose the condition of being a competitive advantage. Then, what we recommend you is to develop your skills and knowledge to the point that you become nonsubstitutable or at least hardly nonsubstitutable in order to leverage the benefits of being a competitive advantage to the company you are working for.

We have always supported the idea of identifying the critical processes in the software companies. It can be done by using MCDM methods, preparing the criteria after gaining the expert views, and then prioritizing the processes based on their weights. Actually, in the companies where the number of distinct processes is not many, all processes can be examined. The aforementioned suggestion is particularly relevant for companies with complex and/or numerous processes. This facilitates the improvement process by zooming in on a certain number of processes of high significance, saving time, effort, and budget and accelerating the progress.

The other noteworthy subject is that the lessons learned are easily forgotten in organizations. Similar mistakes are made again and again. We have always underlined the importance of keeping records of lessons learned in the companies we provide consulting to.

Kaizen, an umbrella concept containing other techniques such as Kanban and Six Sigma, roots back to Japan; it is mainly implemented in manufacturing, targeting the enhancement of situations by continuous efforts performing small improvements where improvement is considered either CI or innovation (Singh & Singh, 2009).

NOTES

As a result of the increasing popularity of the adoption of agile methodologies by many software companies, Kanban has been become a widely used technique like scrum. Unfortunately, the perceived difference between the usages of these two is limited to the columns on their boards, not much more. In many cases, it is the choice of having "to do," "in progress," and "done" columns versus having more detailed ones.

There is a need for the explanation of Kanban as a CI technique to the practitioners in software companies. They may not leverage the benefits of Kanban due to their misperception of the technique.

Sustainable Lean Six Sigma (SLSS) Framework was put forward to increase sustainable manufacturing performance, devised with reference to the DMAIC approach incorporating steps of problem identification, indicator efficiency calculation, analysis, corrective action suggestion, and controlling by means of a check sheet (Marsetiya Utama & Abirfatin, 2023).

NOTES

Six Sigma and its related tools are not adopted by many software companies as far as we see in the firms. We may relate this to two probable reasons:

- *It is perceived to be a complex method probably due to its statistical approach. It will be a matter of preference or the issue is with people not bearing enough knowledge and skills to apply the tools.*
- *The second reason may be the misconception that this method is used solely in manufacturing companies, despite the books and articles accessible on the implementation of Six Sigma in software companies.*

Among the Six Sigma tools, the ones utilized more than the others in software companies are DMAIC and DMADV:

DMAIC and **DMADV** are Six Sigma tools comprising the steps to CI (Purushothaman & Ahmad, 2022). The first comes from the first letters of define, measure, analyze, improve, and control, and the second originates from define, measure, analyze, design, and verify steps.

DMAIC is preferred for solving problems in relation to improving the process, while DMADV is selected for devising or redesigning the processes (Purushothaman & Ahmad, 2022).

5.2 Sustaining the Continuous Improvement

Strengthening our companies in terms of the areas brought in the next information box can be fruitful for sustaining our CI practices.

Key to Sustainable Continuous Improvement (SCI) was mentioned in a precious study as the thorough employee engagement with both physical and emotional commitment of management empowering the employees with training, effective communication, and leveraging Kaizen practices (Costa, et al., 2019).

An interesting study was conducted to see whether characteristics of team members play a role in their behavior concerning sustainability of CI activities, and the results showed that employees' seniority and age affect related team behavior in a positive way (Tortorella et al., Fogliatto, Vergara, Quelhas, & Sawhney, 2021).

In another research, peer learning, change acceptance, awareness, and responsibility within and outside of work has a significant relationship with the perceived impact of Kaizen effects after months of execution (Glover et al., Farris, & Van Aken, 2015).

NOTES

After examining the papers and inspecting the implementation of CI tools in practice, we can realize the significance role of people in sustaining the CI and maintaining it throughout time. By people, we mean managers, external stakeholders, and employees.

Manager's commitment and support are the essential issues here just like their vitality in any kind of quality practices.

External stakeholders play an important role in the continuance of the improvements. Their commitment and support are the drivers, while their ignorance, opposition, or negligence may have a negative impact on sustaining the continuance improvement for the long term, and the further relevant strategies and objectives.

Employees, their behavior, the zest for learning, their persistence in doing the right things even if it is hard, together with their commitment, may all positively have an impact on SCI.

To conclude, granted all mentioned in this chapter and in "Notes" section of the book, sustainable CI is highly dependent on people who formulate the fitted strategies, make commitments to them, and take actions to make them real.

References

Bhuiyan, N., & Baghel, A. (2005). An Overview of Continuous Improvement: From the Past to the Present. *Management Decision*, 43(5), 761–771.

Costa, F., Lispi, L., Staudacher, A. P., Rossini, M., Kundu, K., & Cifone, F. D. (2019). How to Foster Sustainable Continuous Improvement: A Cause-Effect Relations Map of Lean Soft Practices. *Operations Research Perspectives*, 6, 1–12.

Glover, W. J., Farris, J. A., & Van Aken, E. M. (2015). The Relationship between Continuous Improvement and Rapid Improvement Sustainability. *International Journal of Production Research*, 53(13), 4068–4086.

Kaye, M., & Anderson, R. (1999). Continuous Improvement: The Ten Essential Criteria. *International Journal of Quality & Reliability Management*, 16(5), 485–506.

Marsetiya Utama, D., & Abirfatin, M. (2023). Sustainable Lean Six-Sigma: A New Framework for Improve Sustainable Manufacturing Performance. *Cleaner Engineering and Technology*, 17, 1–14.

Purushothaman, K., & Ahmad, R. (2022). Integration of Six Sigma Methodology DMADV Steps with QFD, DFMEA, and TRIZ Applications for Image-Based Automated Inspection System Development: A Case Study. *International Journal of Lean Six Sigma*, 13(6), 1239–1276.

Singh, J., & Singh, H. (2009). Kaizen Philosophy: A Review of Literature. *IUP Journal of Operations Management*, 8(2), 51–72.

Terney, P. B., & Anderson, B. (1989). Accounting for Continuous Improvement. *Sloan Management Review*, 1–11.

Tortorella, G. L., Fogliatto, F. S., Vergara, M. C., Quelhas, G. O., & Sawhney, R. (2021). Influence of Team Members' Characteristics on the Sustainability of Continuous Improvement Initiatives. *Total Quality Management*, 32(7–8), 852–868.

Index

Note: Locators in *italics* represent figures and **bold** indicate tables in the text.

Printed in the United States
by Baker & Taylor Publisher Services